A NATIONAL TRUST

MISCELLANY

THE NATIONAL TRUST'S GREATEST
SECRETS & SURPRISES

IAN ALLEN

Published by National Trust Books
An imprint of HarperCollins Publishers
1 London Bridge Street
London SE1 9GF
www.harpercollins.co.uk

HarperCollins Publishers
1st Floor, Watermarque Building, Ringsend Road, Dublin 4, Ireland

First published 2022

© National Trust Books 2022
Illustrations © August Lamm 2022

ISBN 978-1-91-165743-9

10 9 8 7 6 5 4 3 2 1

If you would like to comment on any aspect of this book, please contact us at
the above address or national.trust@harpercollins.co.uk

National Trust publications are available at National Trust shops or online at
nationaltrustbooks.co.uk

CONTENTS

INTRODUCTION

Welcome to *A National Trust Miscellany*: a smorgasbord of strangely compelling facts and figures about the National Trust.

From its humble beginnings in 1895, the National Trust is now made up of 5.6 million members and about 50,000 volunteers: that's a country the size of Finland and a town the size of Taunton respectively. It looks after about 780 miles of coastline, over 600,000 acres of land and more than 500 buildings – not to mention over a million collection items. Working with its 1,500 tenant farmers, it has become a leading organisation in promoting sustainable agriculture. You probably won't be surprised to hear that the Trust runs 280 cafés, but you might not know that it also cares for 39 pubs. Perhaps you're thinking that an organisation of such scale and scope might have an interesting tale or two to tell. And you'd be right.

A team of experts and researchers at the National Trust, ably led by Amy Feldman, has worked tirelessly to comb its archives and unearth some of its brightest gems for your delight. Not only that, but the volunteers who do so much to help look after National Trust places, and the members whose support is so vital to its work, have been delving into their own richly stocked memory banks for fascinating stories attached to the places they know and love. All of these efforts have enabled me to assemble this captivating cornucopia that's guaranteed to pique your curiosity and have you planning your next Trust visit.

I've been a member of the National Trust for donkey's years, and I'm still finding out new things about it all the time. While I was writing this introduction, even, I learned of the Trust's re-opening, after 20 years, of the world's tallest three-sided obelisk: the magnificent Wellington Monument in Somerset. Following a £3.1 million fundraising campaign and a two-year

A taste for the macabre. A Japanese porcelain tobacco jar from
Agatha Christie's curious collection at Greenway in Devon.

restoration project, you can now experience this extraordinary landmark on a whole new level by climbing all 232 steps to the top of its 53m (173ft) tower. And in case the breathtaking views at the top aren't reward enough, you'll also receive a badge as a memento upon your descent.

In this book you'll find intriguing snippets about the Trust's historic houses, its lovingly tended gardens and wild outdoor spaces. There are tales of royalty, art, sport and even modern(ish) technology. You'll journey under the floorboards of houses, meet weird and wonderful characters, and discover some of the strange jobs assigned to National Trust staff. Pit your wits against the Trust curators and try to identify some of the most mysterious objects in their care. Immerse yourself in tantalising trivia. What was the scale of the pigeon poop problem at Wimpole's Folly? What did Rudyard Kipling mean by the secret code in his guestbook at Bateman's? Which are the Trust's top ten toilets? And where do you have to take your life in your hands, just to do a spot of weeding? Read on to unearth the answers to all these questions and many, many more …

CHAPTER 1

AROUND THE HOUSES

HAWKER'S HUT

One of the smallest properties in the care of the National Trust is a tiny hut built into a Cornish cliff by Victorian cleric Reverend Robert Hawker using timbers from shipwrecks. Hawker was also a poet – penning Cornwall's unofficial anthem, 'Trelawny' (1824) – and he came here to write, as well as smoke opium and look out for sailors in distress. Described as 'a coast life-guard in a cassock', if the clergyman failed to save them, he at least made sure they had a decent Christian burial.

HIDDEN GEMS

Priest Holes

In the Elizabethan era, tiny hiding places were built in many great houses to shelter Roman Catholic priests from persecution. **Baddesley Clinton** in Warwickshire has two of these 'priest holes': one above a cupboard in the bedroom and a drain in the corner of the kitchen. Anticipating *The Shawshank Redemption* by about 400 years, access to the latter was through a shaft from the garderobe (medieval toilet) above.

Coughton Court (also in Warwickshire) has a cunning 'double hide', giving the priest extra protection: if anyone stumbled upon the first section, they'd be out of luck, as the priest would be safely squirrelled away in an even more hidden, second cubbyhole.

Secret Doors
Oxburgh Hall in Norfolk has seven hidden doors including one within a wall of bookcases in the library, decorated with real book spines sporting tongue-in-cheek titles that refer to people and events from Oxburgh's long history.

Buried Bathtub
Are you fed up of being interrupted by the kids while you're trying to have a long wallow in the bath? Take a leaf out of Lord Curzon's book, who concealed his en suite inside a cupboard at **Montacute House**, Somerset.

Murder Holes
Men slept in the corner towers of **Chirk Castle**, near Wrexham, which also doubled up as defence spots. Each one came complete with a 'murder hole' on every floor next to the entrance, where they'd lie in wait, ready to drop stones or fire arrows on would-be invaders. You can still see them (the murder holes, not the defending army) in the Adam Tower.

Secret Passages
A set of hidden tunnels unwinds beneath **Calke Abbey** in Derbyshire, leading to the cellars, brewhouse and some agricultural outbuildings. Others allowed gardeners to get to work without disturbing the family. Now they're less secret, and open for visitors.

REVEREND ROBERT HAWKER (1803-75)

This clergyman, who was quite literally a colourful character – he rejected the normal clerical black for his favourite yellows and purples, and was known to wear a fez on occasions – built what is now one of the smallest properties in the care of the National Trust (see page 8). In a varied ecclesiastical life, he was the originator of harvest festivals, excommunicated a cat for catching a mouse on the Sabbath, and converted to Roman Catholicism on his deathbed. His walking companion was a pig called Gyp, and he was a lover of practical jokes: he once impersonated a mermaid by sitting on Bude breakwater, to the bemusement of onlookers, wearing nothing but a plaited seaweed wig and an oilskin wrap around his legs (perhaps he was the original 'young lady from Bude …' in the cheeky limerick).

ROOMS TO SPARE

One of the largest – if not *the* largest – Trust properties is **Knole** in Kent. No one's even sure how many rooms it has, but it's somewhere around 400 and you could fit about 50 tennis courts on its expanse of roofs.

SMARAGDITE?

Pope Sixtus V had a penchant for excommunicating monarchs, including our own Elizabeth I. He originally owned the Pope's Cabinet – can't think why it's called that – at **Stourhead**, Wiltshire, which dates from around 1585. With its 153 drawers and a design like a church façade, it is one of the most elaborate items cared for by the Trust, and is inlaid with the following exotic and bafflingly obscure gems and elements:

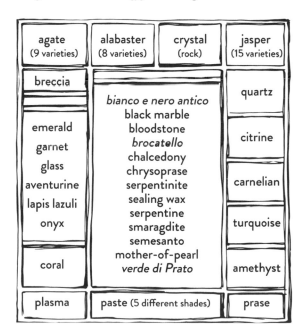

agate (9 varieties)	alabaster (8 varieties)	crystal (rock)	jasper (15 varieties)
breccia			quartz
emerald	*bianco e nero antico*		
garnet	black marble		citrine
glass	bloodstone		
aventurine	*brocatello*		carnelian
lapis lazuli	chalcedony		
onyx	chrysoprase		
	serpentinite		turquoise
	sealing wax		
	serpentine		
coral	smaragdite		amethyst
	semesanto		
	mother-of-pearl		
	verde di Prato		
plasma	paste (5 different shades)		prase

HEY, BIG SPENDER

One of the National Trust's biggest conservation projects to date was preserving **Ightham Mote**, a medieval manor house in Kent. Work began in 1986 and took 20 years, at the cost of £10 million. Not surprisingly, considering the house is surrounded by a moat, one of the many problems encountered was wet rot.

*The number of razors that reputedly used to hang on the wall of the 4th Earl of Lichfield's dressing room at **Shugborough**, Staffordshire. Wonder what he did in a leap year?*

GARGOYLE OR HUNKY PUNK?

Those strange carvings of animal and human figures on the sides of old buildings weren't just put up as decoration: they were intended to protect the building from evil or harmful spirits and, in many cases, acted as waterspouts. If it spouts

water, it's a gargoyle – from the French *gargouille*, meaning 'throat' or 'gullet'. If it doesn't, what you're looking at is technically called a grotesque (also known in Somerset as a hunky punk). They're enough to frighten anyone off. You can find some of the best National Trust gargoyles and grotesques at the Victorian Gothic **Knightshayes Court** in Devon, where William Burges designed the fantastical creatures that adorn the house from his imagination, also adding representations of the seven deadly sins and aspects of medieval life.

HIGH MAINTENANCE

The National Trust Manual of Housekeeping is the Trust's guide to looking after its properties. Hard to put down, it's even harder to pick up, weighing in at 3kg (6½lb) and being 7cm (nearly 3in) thick. Its 928 pages detail the steps staff take to counter the six 'agents of deterioration' that their historic houses are constantly at risk from: humidity, light, pests, dust, mechanical damage and mould. Here's how some of these problems are combatted.

Heat and Humidity

National Trust properties have special 'conservation' heating. The ideal temperature is a little cooler than you'd normally have it at home. This helps maintain just the right humidity levels: high enough so paintings and furniture don't dry and crack, but not so high that mould starts developing.

Light

The Trust doesn't just have a financial budget – many of its historic rooms are subject to a yearly 'light budget' (measured in lux-hours) to protect fabrics and other light-sensitive items from damage. If you've visited a lot of properties you may have noticed the blue wool dosimeters (cards with squares of blue wool that fade according to light exposure), or gone through rooms that are curtained or shuttered to reduce the amount of damaging light that gets in.

Dust

In 2007 the Trust spent roughly £2 per visitor on dusting. It's even helped compile a 'Dust Atlas' to identify different types of dust, how often it should be removed and by what method.

ATTENTION TO DETAIL

Imagine taking apart a 2.4m (8ft) crystal chandelier piece by piece before reassembling it, or spending months painstakingly cleaning decorative pieces with cotton buds. That was the task facing National Trust experts preserving the John Nash roof at **Attingham Park**, Shropshire. The original roof, an ingenious and beautiful early 19th-century mixture of cast iron and glass designed to let natural light into the picture gallery below, had only one flaw – it leaked. In 2014 a weatherproof 'floating' glass roof was installed above the Nash roof to protect it from the elements without detracting from its grandeur.

HEXADECAGONAL HOUSE

The National Trust, you probably won't be surprised to learn, has only one 16-sided property in its portfolio. **A la Ronde** in Devon was built in the late 18th century by cousins Jane and Mary Parminter to showcase souvenirs from their Grand Tour of Europe; it was partly inspired by the 6th-century Basilica of San Vitale in Ravenna, Italy.

You can choose which door to take out of the Octagon Room (there are eight, in case you hadn't guessed), you can even tinkle on the grand piano, but one place you can't enter is the amazing Shell Gallery, where 25,000 shells adorn the walls in a stunning artistic display. It's so fragile it's been closed to visitors for over 20 years, but now everyone can get a flavour from an interactive video.

COLOSSAL CARPET

When the carpet at **Cragside**, Northumberland, needed a full clean, naturally the Trust called in a car mechanic, who advised on how best to jack up the heavy rollers used to remove the

massive floor covering, which had a very complex structure.
Let's hope they washed their hands …

CURIOUS CHARACTERS

MARY PARMINTER
(1767–1849)

Mary was a remarkable woman who, from the age of 17, spent ten years touring Europe with her cousin Jane at a time when the Grand Tour was mainly the preserve of men. They returned to England bursting with ideas and built A la Ronde (see page 15) inspired by their visit to the 16-sided Basilica of San Vitale in Ravenna. Never marrying herself, Mary stipulated in her will that A la Ronde should only be inherited by single female relatives, each of whom would have to give it up if they married. They ran out of eligible candidates within three decades, and the house had its first male owner in 1886.

STATE OF THE ART?

Castle Drogo in Devon is the most recent castle to have been built in England, begun in 1911 and completed in 1930, so the least you'd expect is that it would keep the rain out – but the roof was leaking even before building was finished. Recent restoration work has finally fixed the problem, but it was a mammoth task, involving:

- Over **3,500 blocks** of stone weighing up to **1.4 tonnes** each being removed and given unique markings so they could be reset in their original position later.
- **913 windows** being removed, restored and resealed.
- **40 miles** of stonework being completely repointed.

HOW MANY TRUST VOLUNTEERS DOES IT TAKE TO CHANGE A LIGHT BULB?

To be honest, no one's completely sure, but assuming one to hold the ladder and another to change the bulb, you'd need 18,000 people to change the estimated 9,000 light bulbs the Trust has to replace every year.

SAVE OUR SOLES

When contractors working for the Trust at **Gelli Iago,** a remote Snowdonian cottage, were repairing a chimney in 2010, they made a strange discovery – almost a hundred individual 19th-century shoes. It seems unlikely that the residents could have mislaid so many items of footwear, so the superstition that concealed shoes were thought to offer protection from evil spirits provides one explanation. However, they do appear to have needed rather a lot …

HOUSE MUSIC

The discovery by the Trust of a diary on 1 April 2019 at **Osterley House,** London, apparently revealed it as the home of the world's first 'night-club', where loud music was played, copious amounts of gin imbibed and one might witness 'ladies dancing in a circle around their reticules'.

GOING UP ...

You wouldn't want to have to polish some of the items in the Trust's collections, and you'd definitely need a head for heights to use the tallest:

16m (52½ft): A ladder found in the cellar of **Chastleton House**, Oxfordshire. Made in 1805, it was long enough for an intrepid workman to carry out glass and gutter maintenance on the fifth floor of the Oxfordshire country house. It had to be raised up by pulling one end with ropes to the top of the house, while gently adjusting the angle from the bottom.

11m-plus (36ft): An oak dining table at **Knole**, Kent; this one was extended in the 18th century. It was mostly used by the household's servants.

8.4m (27½ft): An oak dining table from around 1630 at **Hardwick Hall**, Derbyshire. Two of the wooden planks stretch the entire length of the table. It's accompanied by benches made from single 5.8m (19ft) planks.

HAUNTED HOUSES

Where better to find ghosts than in some of the oldest and most historic houses in the country?

Aberconwy House, *Conwy*

If you're visiting Wales's oldest townhouse (built around 1420), keep your nostrils peeled for the scent of pipe tobacco and flowers. This often precedes the appearance of a Victorian gentleman who ran it as a temperance (alcohol-free) hotel in the 19th century.

GUESS
THE ITEM

Answer on page 25.

Blickling Hall, *Norfolk*

The hall stands upon the site of a former medieval manor, thought to be the birthplace of Henry VIII's second wife, Anne Boleyn, who was beheaded on 19 May 1536. It's said that each year she returns to Blickling on the anniversary of her death with her head placed upon her lap, driven up to the house in a coach drawn by a similarly headless horseman.

Clouds Hill, *Dorset*

T. E. Lawrence, better known as Lawrence of Arabia, adored his cottage here. He died nearby in a motorcycle accident, and ever since people have reported seeing a figure in Arab dress entering his home at dusk.

Croft Castle, *Herefordshire*
The spooks in the Midlands' (allegedly) most haunted house are thought to include Owain Glyndŵr, the Welsh freedom fighter from whom the Croft family is descended.

Dunstanburgh Castle, *Northumberland*
Thomas, 2nd Earl of Lancaster, was beheaded as a traitor in 1322. His executioner appears to have been having an off day – it took several strikes before the job was complete. It's said that a horror-struck Earl still walks the grounds of the castle he built, bearing his decapitated head.

Felbrigg Hall, *Norfolk*
If you see the spectre of William Windham III in the library here, don't worry. He's thought to be returning to read the many books he acquired during his busy life as a politician.

Ham House, *Surrey*
This 17th-century mansion is reputed to be the most haunted place cared for by the National Trust. Among the 15 ghosts is Leone Sextus Tollemache, who supposedly appeared in his beloved cherry garden the very morning he was killed in France in the First World War.

Treasurer's House, *York*
The site of the oldest ghosts in Britain: a spectral Roman legion that an unsuspecting heating engineer reportedly witnessed trooping through the basement. Strangely, only their top halves were visible as they were marching lower than the floor. Later excavations revealed a Roman road once ran through the site of the house, about 45cm (18in) below the cellar's floor level.

SUPER-SIZED KENNEL

We all like to spoil our pets, but don't let your pooch see the dog kennel at **Ightham Mote,** Kent, or he'll get extremely jealous. The 2m (6½ft) high house was constructed in 1891 specially for Dido the St Bernard to sleep in. Its next two occupants, two Pekingese, probably found it a bit on the roomy side. The kennel is now Grade I listed, bringing a whole new meaning to the phrase 'in the doghouse'.

ODD ONE OUT

Which one of these is the odd one out, and why?

A: Lord Nuffield's appendix
B: Mary Anne Disraeli's foot
C: Henry Paget's leg

Answer:

A: Lord Nuffield's appendix is the only real body part. Henry Paget's leg, on display at **Plas Newydd**, Anglesey, is an artificial one that replaced the real one he lost at the Battle of Waterloo. A marble cast of Mary Anne Disraeli's left foot sits on what was her Prime Minister husband's desk at **Hughenden,** Buckinghamshire. The appendix of motor-car designer Lord Nuffield is his actual appendix (pickled, naturally), brought home by him after his operation and now residing in a cupboard at **Nuffield Place**, Oxfordshire.

WITCH MARKS

If you couldn't afford one of the gargoyles or grotesques described earlier to ward off demons and evil spirits (see page 12), a simpler alternative was to scratch a witch mark into your stately home, cattle barn or hovel. Most date from the medieval period up to around the 1730s, when fear of witches began to diminish.

The marks tend to be made up of intersecting lines, creating a web or mesh that would confuse or trap a demon to prevent it from entering a home. You also find overlapping 'V's, known as Marian marks, which are thought to form the Virgin Mary's initials. Here are the best National Trust places to find witch marks:

Knole, Kent: King James I had a keen interest in witchcraft and witch-hunting, so maybe that's why Thomas Sackville, Lord Treasurer, made sure that the beams and joists above the ceiling of the King's Room, where he intended the monarch to sleep on his visits, had a plethora of witch marks (or maybe they were just added by a superstitious labourer). But Sackville died in 1608 before building work was finished, and James never did visit Knole. So we never got to find out witch marks worked and witch marks didn't ...

Belton House, Lincolnshire: The stables, dating from 1688, bear over 500 historic graffiti inscriptions, including apotropaic markings in the form of Marian marks, compass-drawn designs, and a rare Auseklis cross **(below).**

Bodiam Castle, East Sussex: Witch marks can be found among the inscriptions that cover almost every entrance and window.

Clandon Park, Surrey: Investigations undertaken following the fire in 2015 have revealed witch marks on walls in a basement room, and an interlocking 'V' and 'M' representing the Virgin Mary on a re-used timber beam in the Speakers' Parlour.

CROOME'S RELIGIOUS PAST

The 18th-century **Croome Court** in Worcestershire was bought by the Roman Catholic Church in 1948, and run as a boys' school by nuns until 1979, when it was purchased by the Hare Krishna movement. During this time the Dining Room was repainted in vibrant colours that can still be seen today. It turned out the movement had overstretched its resources, however, and they moved out five years later. The Trust took over its care in 2007.

GOLD MINE
MANAGER

Commercial operations at Dolaucothi Gold Mines in Carmarthenshire ended in 1938, and it was during this period that the old Roman workings were discovered; it remains the only known Roman gold mine in Britain. The site was donated to the Trust in 1941 and requires a mine manager by law. Nowadays they must have a mine supervisor qualification, and are judged on conservation and tourist development, rather than how much gold they can extract. Visitors are given a guided underground tour and then can pan for gold themselves and try to strike it rich.

WHAT LINKS THESE CHARACTERS?

- Bill Stickers
- Sister Agatha
- The Nark
- Red Biddy
- The Bludy Beershop
- Shot Biddy

Answer:

No, they're not Grand National winners. If you know your National Trust history, you might recognise them as the Trust's answer to Robin Hood and his Merry Men, the notorious Ferguson's Gang. These six determined and wealthy women got together in 1927 with a ruthless plan to donate money to the National Trust in the most surreal ways possible, including stuffing money inside fake pineapples and cigars. On one occasion a mask-wearing gang member burst into the office of the Trust's treasurer and forced the poor chap to accept £100. What scoundrels! Over a two-decade period their reign of terror enabled the Trust to save many properties and locations for the nation, including **Shalford Mill** (Surrey), **Newtown Old Town Hall** (Isle of Wight), and the **Mayon** and **Trevescan** cliffs (Cornwall).

GUESS THE ITEM ANSWER

If you were told the metal pot was for filling with hot charcoal, you'd be forgiven for assuming it's some ingenious sledge-like contraption that stops you getting frostbite in your feet while you're enjoying winter sports. But it's actually a bed warmer from **Felbrigg Hall** in Norfolk. Between the chances of your bedsheets catching fire and the lovely smell of charcoal to waft you to sleep, you might think a cold bed would be a better option.

UNDER THE FLOORBOARDS

Whenever the Trust has to carry out a bit more maintenance than your average spruce up, it seems it can't resist having a ferret under the floorboards to see what might have dropped down there in years gone by. Here are the National Trust's Seven Wonders of the Woodwork:

1 Two Mummified Rats
Step forward – hang on, that might be difficult – Martin and Collin, named after the pair who discovered them at **Dyrham Park**, South Gloucestershire. During the Second World War the house was run as a nursery for evacuated children, which probably explains why other recent underground finds there include a toy panda, a wooden dog and some chocolate tins.

2 A Georgian Shoe
And what's so interesting about that? Well, it's thought this particular find at **Wimpole** in Cambridgeshire was not mislaid but placed there deliberately as a charm against evil spirits, like a cobbler's witch mark. Either that or a Georgian child was playing a practical joke on dear Papa …

3 A 1970s TIME CAPSULE

The Trust must have been excited to learn what historical gems it would discover when it carried out a two-year re-servicing project at 18th-century **Croome Court** in Worcestershire. In the end staff turned up a few period nails and a single leather shoe. They did find quite a bit from the contractors who'd carried out work there in the 1970s, though: a wallpaper brush, old newspapers, several cigarette packets and a magazine. Handily, they also found a list giving the companies and addresses of some of the decorators, so they'll be able to get their stuff back.

4 *Star Trek* Doors

Move over, USS *Enterprise*, the builders at **Kingston Lacy** in Dorset were way ahead of you. Anticipating those space-age swishing doors by several centuries, when the floorboards were lifted in the saloon of this 17th-century country house conservators found the remains of a chain-and-cog system that used to be linked to the double doors. This would have enabled both doors to open simultaneously and smoothly just by gentle pressure on one of them, making it much easier for servants bearing trays to enter safely.

5 Message in a Bottle

In 2017 archaeologists at **Knole** in Kent were surveying under the attic floorboards when they found a bottle of Perrier water (by appointment to Edward VII, no less) containing paper and a note in the top urging the finder to 'Take this out and see inside'. What would it reveal? A mislaid *aide mémoire*, perhaps ('Remember to clean under floorboards every ten years')? A discarded souvenir of a seaside trip ('Am marooned on Isle of Sheppey – send help!')? Alas, it was a little more prosaic: 'Sept 26th 1906. This bottle was dropped [sic] here in the year AD 1906 by S. G. Doggett when these radiators were put in, also the Hot Water Service.'

6 Memory Matchbox

A matchbox unearthed at **West Wycombe Park**, Buckinghamshire, was nothing special. But on the bottom of it someone had written in pencil: 'Titanic Sunk April 15th 1912'. Was it someone writing it at the time when they'd just heard about the tragedy? Was it written as a reminder to pass on news of the shipwreck to someone else? Or was it a concealed note to be smuggled into a school exam? It would be fascinating to know.

7 Jewel in the Crown

Saving the best until last, the *crème de la crème* of National Trust floorboard finds has to be **Oxburgh Hall** in Norfolk, where a 2018–21 restoration programme just kept turning up unexpected treasures:

- Two deluxe rats' nests made from over 200 pieces of Tudor and Elizabethan fabric, including silk, velvet, leather, wool and embroidery; nothing but the best for Oxburgh rats.
- A fragment of a pre-Reformation music manuscript.
- An illuminated manuscript page complete with gold leaf, thought to be from a 15th-century Psalter.
- An almost-intact book dated 1569 called *The King's Psalms*, with gilded leather binding.

CHAPTER 2

UP THE GARDEN PATH

SOME LIKE IT HOT

The gardeners of the country estates of yesteryear went to great lengths to keep their plants cosy. The Walled Garden at **Llanerchaeron** in Ceredigion had fruit beds warmed by hypocausts (hot air circulating between double layers of bricks) and garden walls warmed by fire pits. In the gardens at **Wimpole Hall**, Cambridgeshire, the walls were heated by a system of flues in the brickwork, while a canny gardener at Benjamin Disraeli's **Hughenden** country home in Buckinghamshire took a low-tech approach to the problem of cold snaps by creating a gentle south-facing slope that allowed warmer air to rise to where it could be most beneficial, and installing an ingenious 'frost gate' in the bottom corner of the garden to let all the cold air out.

AND NOW, ONE FOR THE GALANTHOPHILES

Which, as I'm sure you don't need explaining, is a snowdrop enthusiast. And they're sure to gather at **Kingston Lacy** in Dorset as over 40 varieties begin to poke their little white heads out in January and February, delighting in names like Ding Dong, Wendy's Gold, Three Ships and – my favourite – Heffalump.

DIZZY DATES

The large earthenware pots containing pear, plum and fig trees in the 1870s Orchard House at **Cragside**, Northumberland, were mounted on turntables so they could be regularly rotated to catch an even amount of sunlight. There was also an elaborate heating system to ensure optimum growing conditions.

DRAGGED KICKING AND SCREAMING INTO THE 19TH CENTURY

These days naming something a Large Lazy Blonde would definitely be frowned upon, but this is just what a certain lettuce variety grown at **Tatton Park**, Cheshire, was dubbed by French gardeners in the 19th century. The walled garden at Tatton Park does not feature anything that couldn't have been grown before 1900, making it a piece of living history.

GRANDAD'S FAVOURITE

And not just Grandad's Favourite – who wouldn't want to visit the National Rhubarb Collection at **Clumber Park**, Nottinghamshire? There are more varieties here than you could shake a stick (of rhubarb, obviously) at – in fact, with over 130, it's the second-largest collection in the world. Can you spot the one below that *isn't* rhubarb, though?

- Hardy Tarty
- Puddle-Duck
- Stockbridge Guardsman
- Glaskin's Perpetual

Answer:

Puddle-Duck is the odd one out, though you can visit the rhubarb patch at Beatrix Potter's **Hill Top**, Cumbria, and see where Jemima Puddle-Duck hid her eggs.

GUESS
THE ITEM

Answer on page 46.

BELIEVE IT OR NUT?

Forgetful red squirrels on **Brownsea Island** in Poole Harbour, Dorset, were given a helping hand by Trust rangers in 2020, as announced on 1 April. Whenever the staff discovered a stash of unclaimed nuts somewhere on the island, they would post little signs pointing the way to them so this endangered species could find their food.

35,000

*The number of flowers in **Cotehele**'s 18m (60ft) long Christmas garland in 2015.*

ATTINGHAM ON THE B-LIST

And there's nothing wrong with that when we're talking about a Regency Grade II-listed bee house at **Attingham Park**, Shropshire. Previously located in the orchard, this impressive structure has been moved to the lawn, south-west of the Kitchen Garden. The designer is not known, but we do know that both John Nash and Humphry Repton produced work for Attingham in the early 19th century, so there's a reasonable chance the bee house had an A-list creator.

GROW YOUR OWN SPONGES

In 2019 National Trust staff at **Knightshayes** in Devon began to grow their own loofahs – *Luffa cylindrica*, a member of the cucumber family – so they could harvest the crop to use as natural sponges in the kitchens; any excess produce was sold online. After this success, in 2021 they launched a 'grow-along' scheme to encourage more people to grow their own at home and do their bit for the environment. If you fancy having a go, you can find all the instructions you need online. It doesn't say anything about using them to wash your back in the bath, though.

ROYAL ROOSTERS

You can see **Chartwell**'s hen house in the walled garden, much like the one the Churchills had, which they dubbed 'Chickenham Palace'.

WHERE THERE'S MUCK THERE'S HORSE BRASS

In 2014, the National Trust dredged the North Park View pond at **Hare Hill** in Cheshire. It did the pond no end of good but the mechanical diggers used couldn't help making a heck of a mess of the surrounding ground. So four years later, when the other ponds in the woodland garden needed around 2m (6½ft) of sludge removing, it turned to a more traditional kind of horsepower. Jasper and Bolero, the equine muscle of a Cumbrian horse-logging team, spent three weeks removing the muck from the ponds and, as an added bonus and without being asked, contributed some useful manure for the gardens.

HOW MANY TRUST GARDENERS DOES IT TAKE TO CHANGE A TULIP BULB?

You may remember learning in Chapter 1 (see page 17) that the Trust changes 9,000 light bulbs every year. Well, their gardeners would not be impressed by that. The green-fingered gang at **Stowe** in Buckinghamshire plant over 10,000 garden bulbs every year. And, in autumn 2018, a staggering 500,000 (that's right, half a million) were planted at **Ham House** in Richmond.

ABSEILING GARDENER

St Michael's Mount castle in Cornwall, near Land's End, has a walled garden that has been designed to be viewed from above – in fact, a whacking 61m (200ft) above, from the castle terrace. This presents its own challenges, but it's nothing to the task of keeping the rock face between the castle and the garden weed-free, which can only be done by a harnessed horticulturalist with a head for heights and a lot of rope. They abseil down the face, weeding as they go, and once they reach the bottom they have to choose whether to climb back up or take a ten-minute walk back to the castle. Understandably, these extreme weeders are gradually trying to replace invasive plants with species like colourful, trailing *Lampranthus* to make the rockface both more attractive and easier to maintain.

15,500

*Square metres of yew and box hedging at **Powis Castle**, including 14m (46ft) high terraces, which have been there for about 300 years.*

TOP TOPIARY

MOST TIME-CONSUMING TRIMS
Montacute House, *Somerset*
Wibbly wobbly hedges:
3 gardeners, 2 months

Bodnant Garden, *Conwy*
Laburnum Arch:
2 gardeners, 1 month

Powis Castle, *Powys*
Box hedge: 2 gardeners, 6 weeks
Yew hedge: 2 gardeners, 12 weeks
14m (46ft) terraces: 1 gardener, 10 weeks in a cherry-picker

MOST UNUSUAL HEDGE SHAPES
Westwood Manor, *Wiltshire*
A topiary cottage

Blickling, *Norfolk*
Grand pianos

Mount Stewart, *County Down*
Harp, complete with strings
Jumping horse **(below)**

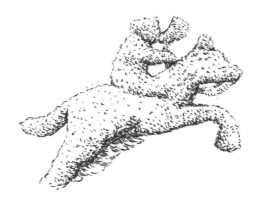

ANY COLOUR YOU LIKE, AS LONG AS IT'S NOT YELLOW

Go and admire the replanted rose gardens at **Dudmaston Estate** in Shropshire; you'll find varieties named after Gertrude Jekyll (who designed a garden at **Lindisfarne Castle,** Northumberland), Octavia Hill (one of the founders of the National Trust) and even Abraham Darby, who was an ancestor of Lady Labouchere, who originally planted the garden at Dudmaston in 1996, the year she died. But you won't find any yellow roses … she *really* didn't like them.

PIRATES, PILFERING AND THE PLANT-HUNTERS

Plant-hunting might not sound like an extreme pursuit, but Georgian, Victorian and Edwardian botanists couldn't just pop down to their local garden centre. They travelled to the world's remotest places to bring back specimens.

- Robert Fortune, who learned Mandarin, disguised himself as a Chinese peasant and survived attacks by pirates on the return voyage to bring back specimens for **Biddulph Grange Garden** in Staffordshire.
- Ernest Wilson got his 'Lily Limp' when caught in an avalanche during his search for the *Lilium regale* in China, which he brought back to **Bodnant Garden**, Conwy.
- Mary Eleanor Bowes inherited **Gibside** following the death of her father in 1760. In spite of a tempestuous private life, she found time to commission plant collector William Paterson to collect plants for her during his expeditions to the Cape of Good Hope, and develop the gardens at Gibside.
- George Maw, long-term tenant at **Benthall Hall**, Shropshire, was dubbed 'the man who labelled Kew'. Maw made his fortune as a tile manufacturer, and in addition to bringing countless specimens of plants back to Benthall for cultivation, he designed and manufactured plant labels for Kew Gardens.

DOCKET DETECTORISTS

When you're trying to find missing plants, your first thought probably isn't to use a metal detector. But at **Bodnant Garden**, of the over 300 hybrid rhododendron varieties that have been registered to the property over the years, only just over 100 have been identified. Some have probably died off, but some are almost certainly lurking in the borders, waiting to be pinned down. So the team there have been working with local detectorists to try and find the metal labels the plants would originally have had attached to them.

FRUITY FUN

There are some weird and wonderful names for heritage varieties grown in the garden at **Knightshayes** in Devon. Can you identify any of these?

- Auntie Madge's Plum Cherry
- Banana Legs
- Box Car Willie
- Charlie Chaplin
- Mr Stripey
- Radiator Charlie's Mortgage Lifter
- Trucker's Favourite
- Yellow Submarine
- Kellogg's Breakfast
- Jelly Bean
- Green Zebra
- Granny's Throwing

Answers:

Well, apologies for a bit of a trick question – they're *all* oddly named tomatoes, just a few of the 200 varieties grown at Knightshayes on a five-year rotation. (And yes, tomatoes are fruits, because they form a flower and contain seeds. As the saying goes, 'Knowledge is knowing tomatoes are fruits; wisdom is not putting them in a fruit salad.')

ENTRANCE ON THE FIRST FLOOR ...

Wightwick Manor just outside Wolverhampton has a cat flap on the first floor that Lady Mander's feline used to access by climbing up the wisteria.

FANTASTIC FERN

There's an *Osmunda* fern at **Colby Woodland Garden** in
Pembrokeshire that, with a 6m (19½ft) circumference, is
thought to be the UK's largest, and around 400 years old. It
would have been a big attraction for pteridomaniacs (that's fern
fanciers to you and me) in Victorian times – there was a craze
for the plants, and images of them adorned everything from
teapots to chamberpots. You can still see a lasting legacy of this
fern-fascination every time you eat a custard cream **(above)**.

A BIT OF HERMIT HISTORY

What does the word hermit conjure up for you today? A solitary
holy man? Someone who's just happiest in their own company?
There are hermitages at several National Trust locations, mostly
added by 18th-century landowners who fancied somewhere to
put their feet up while inspecting their estates.

- The Trust's oldest hermit connection is probably **Inner
  Farne**, off Northumberland, to where St Cuthbert
  withdrew in the 7th century.
- Not all hermits remained in holy contemplation – in the
  1300s, Nicholas de Legh acted as a forerunner to the
  South Foreland Lighthouse that would be built 500 years

later by hanging a lantern near his cave to warn ships.

- In the early 21st century Staffordshire Council revived the 18th-century practice of employing 'ornamental hermits' to look moody and mysterious by hiring someone to spend two days in the hermitage at Great Haywood cliffs at **Shugborough**, Staffordshire.
- The rustic-looking hermitage at **Kedleston Hall** in Derbyshire used to boast a mahogany tea table, presumably so the estate owners could contemplate in comfort.
- An outbuilding in the grounds of **Killerton**, Devon, is known as the Bear Hut because it once housed a black bear called Tom; but its stained-glass window reveals its former life as a hermitage.

'I CALL THAT ONE SUDOKU ...'

The first monkey puzzle trees were imported from South America in 1795, a few seeds being put in a doggy-bag by plant collector Archibald Menzies when he was served some at a dinner in Chile. James Bateman (1811–97) at the wonderful **Biddulph Grange Garden** in Staffordshire loved his monkey puzzle trees so much he gave all of them a name, and there is still a dramatic collection of them there today. Four specimens spend ten or so years in the monkey puzzle parterre before being dug up and moved to what has become a magical monkey puzzle forest.

EUROPE'S LARGEST ROCKERY?

The Rock Garden at **Cragside**, Northumberland, is certainly one of the largest, covering 4 acres and surrounding the house – who needs a moat when you've got rocks? It's almost entirely artificial and it's said Lady Armstrong paid the Victorian villagers to bring buckets of fertile soil to create planting pockets. In 2016 a new temporary water feature was added – but not by the Trust – when constant heavy rain created a beautiful cascade, cutting its way through the rockery.

CURIOUS CHARACTERS

EDITH, LADY LONDONDERRY (1878-1959)

The gardens that Lady Londonderry created for Mount Stewart, her family home in County Down, are as exuberant as her imagination. Not many feature a Shamrock Garden, a Dodo Terrace and steps down to a pond designed specially for a Pekingese. In 1915 she formed the Ark, an invitation-only social club where all members were given an alliterative name from nature or mythology – Edith was Circe the Sorceress. A painting by Edmund Brock ('Brock the Badger') of *Circe and the Sirens* hangs at Mount Stewart.

WHO NEEDS ROCKS?

We've all heard of rockeries, but have you heard of stumperies? These weirdly beautiful creations are made of dead tree stumps replanted upside down and were originally designed less as an artwork and more as a scaffold around which other plants (particularly ferns – remember pteridomania? – see page 40) could grow. The first one was created at **Biddulph Grange Garden**, Staffordshire, in 1856 and is still there. It inspired many others, notably in the woods at Prince Charles's Highgrove Estate, although not everyone was impressed. When Prince Philip first saw it, he allegedly asked his son, 'When are you going to set fire to this lot?'

'THE OMNIPOTENT MAGICIAN'

This was how the English poet William Cowper elegantly referred to Lancelot 'Capability' Brown (1716–83) in a work published two years after the remarkable landscape gardener's death. He worked on the grounds of 18 National Trust properties, from **Wallington** (Northumberland) to **Wimpole** (Cambridgeshire). His ubiquitous influence can perhaps be summarised with a barbed quote from one of his contemporaries, another poet, Richard Owen Cambridge:

> *'I hope I die before Capability Brown, so that I may see heaven before it is "improved".'*

AMAZING MAZES

The Trust cares for a large collection of these outdoor puzzles that delight young and old:

For Beginners

If you're really worried about not being able to find your way out, why not start with the pavement maze at **Greys Court**, Oxfordshire. From time to time the Trust even cuts a maze into the grass for a bit of fun, as it did recently at **Powis Castle** (Powys) and **Benthall Hall** (Shropshire).

Intricate Mazes

Speke Hall on Merseyside has a maze with 12 gates, five bridges, four finger mazes, three weather vanes and a tower.

Lost Mazes

Trust staff at **Lyveden Manor** in Northamptonshire didn't realise there used to be a Tudor labyrinth in the grounds until the early 2000s, when someone was looking at some old aerial reconnaissance photographs taken by the US Air Force during the Second World War. From the air the outline was apparent. Historic England was so impressed it immediately awarded the garden Grade I-listed status.

For Spectators

The maze at **Glendurgan Garden** in Cornwall is set on one side of a valley, so less intrepid visitors can sit on the other side and enjoy watching everyone trying to find their way to the thatched summerhouse in the centre. It's not as easy as it looks. Why not try your hand below.

FANTASTIC FACTS ABOUT GLENDURGAN MAZE

- It takes five staff and five volunteers one day to trim the cherry laurel that forms the maze.
- The maze features 650m (2,132ft) of path.
- The design was based on a (now-lost) maze at Sydney Gardens in Bath.
- In 2033 the maze will celebrate its 200th birthday.
- The maze was installed by Alfred Fox to amuse his 12 children.
- Alfred would fine any desperate or cheating child who broke through the hedges in the maze a whole shilling.

THE MOST FAMOUS BRICKLAYER IN THE WORLD

Many of the bricks in the walled garden at **Chartwell**, Kent, were laid between 1925 and 1932 by none other than Sir Winston Churchill. When news of his hobby was reported in the press, the Amalgamated Union of Building Trade Workers wrote inviting him to become a member. Sir Winston Churchill eventually agreed, and applied, but when news of *this* broke there was a backlash from some members and his subscription cheque was never banked.

DEER AND GOOSE

The grounds of **Dunham Massey** in Greater Manchester have two unusual features: a substantial *patte d'oie* (goose's foot) radiating layout of avenues, and its original brick salters (or 'deer leaps') that enabled deer to jump down into the grounds but prevented them from leaving.

LONDON CALLING

Shaw's Corner in Hertfordshire was the home of playwright George Bernard Shaw from 1906 until his death in 1950. His writing hut in the garden is on a rotating base so he could change the light and shade as he desired. He called the hut 'London', so that if he didn't want to be disturbed anyone in the main house could truthfully turn down any enquiries with, 'I'm afraid Mr Shaw is in London'.

GUESS THE ITEM ANSWER

Don't feel bad if you didn't guess that it's a cucumber straightener – the Trust itself once had this catalogued as an ear trumpet! It was invented by the great engineer George Stephenson (1781–1848), a keen gardener who took great pride in his cucumbers.

THE NATIONAL TRUST AT WAR

From the English Civil War to the Cold War, National Trust places have a long history of being used in times of conflict.

KEEP IT UNDER YOUR HAT

Isn't it great when you find a bit of chocolate you'd forgotten you had? In 2021, the National Trust at **Oxburgh Hall** in Norfolk did just that when staff looked inside a Boer War helmet in the attic and discovered a completely intact chocolate bar from 1900, still in its original tin. It was part of a batch commissioned by Queen Victoria to boost morale among the troops, bearing the inscriptions 'South Africa 1900' and 'I wish you a happy New Year'. This one was presumably a memento kept by the 8th Baronet, who was a major in the militia of the King's Liverpool Regiment during the war, and obviously not a chocoholic.

DON'T FIRE UNTIL YOU SEE THE WHITES OF THEIR COWS

The White Park cattle on the **Dinefwr** estate in Carmarthenshire are rarer than giant pandas and had been chewing the cud there continuously for over a thousand years (the book of Hywel the Good mentions them in AD 920) when legend has it that the Second World War forced them to be temporarily relocated as it was feared that German bombers were using their blackout-busting white skins as location-finding aids. Other versions of the story say the poor animals were merely camouflaged with green paint, which caused the confused cattle to see one another as intruders, leading to a mass cow brawl.

PINPOINT ACCURACY

Hughenden in Buckinghamshire was home to a secret unit of mapmakers in the Second World War. Architects, artists, graphic designers and even cartoonists were drafted in for their special skills to create accurate, detailed maps for Bomber Command to use over Germany and Nazi-occupied territory. After the war, operation Hillside, as it had been called, remained top secret and all traces of it at Hughenden were removed. It wasn't until 2004, when a Trust volunteer overheard a visitor telling his grandson about his mapmaking days there, that the facts were revealed, beginning a painstaking detective trail that finally resulted in a permanent display at the property telling its wartime secrets. Although they knew they were helping defeat Hitler, some of the mapmakers acknowledged the human cost: one, Kathleen Hudson, poignantly observed, 'With our paintbrushes we had helped to kill people we did not know.'

THANKS A BUNCH

During the English Civil War, the impregnable **Corfe Castle** in Dorset was home to the Royalist Bankes family. Sir John Bankes was summoned to attend the king in Oxford, and left Corfe in the care of his wife Mary, their servants and a fighting force of just five men. When Parliamentary soldiers arrived in 1643 and demanded its surrender, Mary told them where to go

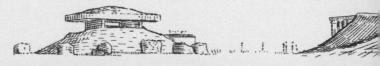

and continued to defy them for three years, repelling all attacks and inflicting significant casualties on the Roundheads, mainly by pouring hot embers on them from Corfe's walls. Finally, in 1646, an act of treachery allowed the Parliamentarians to gain access to the castle through deception. The fortress was captured, and later reduced to a ruin to prevent it being defended again. Lady Mary, however, had the keys to the castle returned to her in recognition of her valiant defence.

WATCH YOUR STEP

These strange-looking structures (below) at what is now Orford Ness National Nature Reserve in Suffolk are a relic from the Cold War. They were a test centre for the environmental impacts of various aspects of the UK's nuclear weapons programme. The structures were designed to absorb and dissipate any explosions in the event of an accident. Hints of the area's military history still pepper the reserve – in some spots there are signs warning of 'unexploded ordnance', encouraging visitors to stick to designated routes.

WHEN THE BALLOON CAME DOWN

During the First World War, a German Zeppelin airship returning from a bombing raid over the East End of London was attacked by the Royal Flying Corps (forerunner of the RAF) and forced down. The 200m (656ft) craft crashed at

Copt Hall Marshes in Essex, narrowly missing a farm labourer's cottage. No one was hurt and the German crew set fire to the airship to destroy any technical information, leaving only an eerie metal skeleton that proved quite a tourist attraction for a while.

WHEEZERS AND DODGERS

During the Second World War, the promontory of **Brean Down** in Somerset was used as a test site for the Department of Miscellaneous Weapons Development (nicknamed the Wheezers and Dodgers). Among their baffling devices were:

- An Expendable Noise Maker: Intended to bamboozle enemy acoustic mines, it misfired during testing and destroyed a hen house.
- Bat Bombs: 'So, what we need to defeat the enemy is a bomb containing a thousand hibernating Mexican free-tailed bats, each with a small incendiary device attached …'
- Exploding Rats: Carcasses filled with plastic explosive.
- Bouncing Bombs: The water-skipping, dam-busting bombs were tested to see if they could attack battleships.

RACE TO THE BAR

When British and Canadian airmen were billeted at **Beningbrough Hall**, North Yorkshire, during the Second World War, the Dressing Room became a makeshift bar – you can still see the scratch marks in the closet where a counter was installed for payment. It was a place where the crews could relax and let off steam. If you could make it from the counter, along the hall, up the stairs, back down and return to the bar in under a minute you qualified for a free pint – leading to at least one enterprising airman attempting it on a motorbike!

CHAPTER 3

THE
GREAT
OUTDOORS

DISAPPEARING DUNES

The National Trust had a tough job on its hands when it took over the running of a stretch of beach at **Formby Point** on Merseyside in 1967 – but tidal erosion means there is now less to look after than when it started. In fact, back then the coastline was 160m (525ft) further out than it is now, making it the fastest-changing coastline in the care of the Trust. In a single tide during storms in the winter of 2013–14, 10m (33ft) of coast disappeared.

UNUSUAL NATIONAL TRUST JOBS

TERN STYLIST

The Farne Islands, Northumberland, are home to a wonderful array of wildlife, including seals, Arctic terns and, of course, puffins. Two full-time rangers spend nine months of the year on the islands monitoring the fauna and carrying out research. When the post was advertised in 2017, would-be applicants were enticed by the promise of frequent storms, no running water and the prospect of being dive-bombed by angry terns protecting their nests. Apparently, one of the tasks the rangers often find themselves doing is blow-drying sickly Arctic tern chicks to keep them alive.

Miles of coast looked after
by the National Trust.

CARRY ON SUNBATHING

A stretch of beach at **Studland**, Dorset, is the Trust's only designated naturist beach to date, where clothes are optional. Walkers are given plenty of warning that 'naturists may be seen' as they approach the beach, and there's an alternative path for those wishing to avoid any embarrassing encounters.

MOST VISITED

Giant's Causeway in County Antrim is regularly at the top of the National Trust attendance charts, with around a million visitors in a typical year coming to see the 40,000 interlocking basalt columns. In 2015, a group of 150 knitters came together to create a giant pair of pants with a 430cm (170in) waist for Finn McCool, the legendary builder of the causeway.

HOW DO THEY KEEP THOSE CLIFFS SO WHITE?

By doing nothing, basically. Although the Trust carries out loads of conservation work on our coastlines, the **White Cliffs of Dover** stay that way because natural erosion periodically 'cleans' the cliff face of plants. In places where they have been protected from erosion, plants will colonise the cliffs and make them green.

THANK GOODNESS IT'S ONLY TWICE A YEAR

In case some people didn't appreciate the huge effort involved, on 1 April 2016 the Trust posted a video showing the elaborate job of moving the massive stones forward an hour at **Avebury Stone Circle**, Wiltshire, in the last weekend of March so the prehistoric sundial would still be accurate as we moved into British Summer Time.

I SPY DINOSAURS

'Take nothing but photographs, leave nothing but footprints', is a good maxim to go by in the countryside. They didn't take any photos, but at Keates Quarry on the **Spyway** in Dorset you can see the footprints dinosaurs left 140 million years ago, only discovered in 1997. Given the number and size of prints preserved, it's thought the site was a watering hole for brachiosaurs, which weighed five times as much as an elephant.

PREHISTORIC HOLIDAYMAKERS

While we're on the subject of footprints, a walk along the sands of **Formby Point** in Merseyside at low tide may reveal 8,000-year-old human footprints baked into the mud and then preserved in sediment beds. To be fair, our ancestors were probably more interested in hunting than soaking up the rays – other prints you might see are those of boar, deer and aurochs (a huge wild ox).

ISLAND LIFE
Lindisfarne Castle, *Northumberland*
Plan your visit to **Lindisfarne Castle** carefully – Holy Island is accessible by causeway only, and is cut off for around six hours, twice a day. Although the tide times are clearly marked, every year several cars are washed away and the occupants have to be either collected by lifeboat or spend hours in a refuge tower. In March 2020, Seahouses RNLI rescued five people, a dog and a wedding dress.

Brownsea Island, *Poole Harbour*
This birthplace of the Scouting and Guiding movement was established as a wildlife refuge by Mary Bonham-Christie after she bought the island in 1927. She evicted residents (who referred to her as the 'Demon of Brownsea'), banned visitors and employed a Danish physical-fitness expert, Bertha Hartung Olsen, to patrol the shores and tip up any boats that tried to land. (Bertha was deported after throwing someone into the sea.) In fairness to Mary, she was motivated by her overwhelming love of animals and her determination that the island should be a natural haven. Her preference for pooches over people was perhaps demonstrated when she put Bryn, the handyman's dog, on the payroll after it cornered five intruders.

Carrick-a-Rede, *County Antrim*
Not for the faint-hearted, there's a 30m (98ft) drop below this rope bridge, opened in 2008. And if you think that sounds precarious, you certainly wouldn't like the original version – comprised only of wooden slats and a single guide rope.

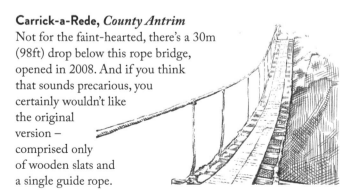

Grasmere Island, *Lake District*
It's just a little island in a lake, very pretty but nothing unusual – you can't even visit it – and the Trust only took over its care in 2017 when it was bequeathed it in a will. Yet its sale in 1893 was one of the triggers for Hardwicke Rawnsley, a local vicar disturbed at the continuing threat to the Lake District from modern development, to form the National Trust with Octavia Hill and Sir Robert Hunter.

Great Mewstone, *Devon*
The South Coast equivalent of Alcatraz, now a nature reserve, was, from 1744, home to a petty criminal who was banished there for seven years – he liked it so much he stayed for the rest of his life. Then, in the early 19th century, another local villain, due to be transported to Australia, haggled his sentence down to exile at Great Mewstone. He would row day-trippers to the island 'in me bote … for two pence appease'.

Lundy, *Bristol Channel*
Lundy means 'Puffin Island' in Old Norse (not to be confused with Anglesey's Puffin Island, which means 'Puffin Island'). Lying about 11 miles off the Devon coast, down the centuries it's been a Celtic settlement, a pirate hideout, a Civil War stronghold and the realm of self-proclaimed 'King' Martin Harman in the 20th century, who produced his own currency and was fined £5 under the Coinage Act. You can now rent one of 23 holiday cottages there for a peaceful retreat.

Northey Island, *Essex*
The Trust cares for several castles, so it is odd that it doesn't have much of an association with battlefields. However, Northey Island is thought to be the site of the pivotal Battle of Maldon in AD 991, where Ethelred the Unready's army was defeated by the Vikings, leading to the imposition of the hated Danegeld, where the Anglo-Saxons paid the Norsemen not to attack them.

Rathlin Island, *County Antrim*

Island Rathlin House Light – whoops, let's start again – Rathlin Island Lighthouse celebrated its 100th anniversary in 2019, and is supposedly the UK's only upside-down lighthouse, situated on Northern Ireland's only inhabited offshore island (population 154 at the last count). It was apparently built that way to cut through the dense, low fog that has a habit of enveloping the island.

St Michael's Mount, *Cornwall*

Another causeway-connected island, but for this one you don't need to worry about losing your car because you're not allowed to take vehicles to the island – you have to walk across. And, unlike Lindisfarne, if you miss the tides, you can just book a boat to visit the stunning castle.

Strangford Lough, *County Down*

For the farmers keeping cows and sheep on the shores of this huge Northern Irish sea loch, all that juicy untouched grass on the islands just offshore is too tempting to resist. For nearly 200 years they've been taking their cattle over by raft for grazing – or sometimes just encouraging them to swim across. The Trust cares for 20 islands on the loch, 12 of which are used for grazing, and the animals transported on a special livestock barge, the *Cuan Brig*.

AND NOW FOR SOMETHING COMPLETELY DIFFERENT

In 2011 the National Trust published a list of Silly Walks – short walks from Trust locations with peculiar names. And although it announced it on 1 April, all the names are for real, including:

- Booby's Bay, Cornwall
- Windy Gap, Surrey
- Cock-up Bridge, Cambridgeshire
- The Nostrils, Isle of Wight
- Scrubby Bottoms, Pembrokeshire

SMALL BEGINNINGS 1
On 29 March 1895, the Trust received its first donation of land. A Mrs Fanny Talbot gifted it **Dinas Oleu,** 4½ acres of hillside overlooking Cardigan Bay and the Llŷn Peninsula in Gwynedd.

GUESS THE ITEM

Answer on page 68.

MILLICAN DALTON
(1867-1947)

When you learn that Millican Dalton spent 20 years living in a cave in Castle Crag in Borrowdale, Cumbria, baking his own bread and making his own clothes, you'd be forgiven for wondering why he wasn't included in the list of hermits earlier (see page 40). But this man was no recluse. A keen camper, the self-styled 'Professor of Adventure' led expeditions in the Lake District, featuring rafting, climbing and 'hair's-breadth escapes', normally while wearing his favourite Tyrolean hat. He rarely accepted cash, preferring to be paid in his beloved Woodbine cigarettes.

WHAT CONNECTS ...?

- A council bin nicknamed 'Pete'
- An oil-covered Mars bar
- A packet of crisps from 1976
- Russian fly spray
- An entire picnic from the 1980s

- A Canadian research buoy
- A set of sonar equipment from Texas

Answer:

These are just a few of the weird and worrying things that have washed up on National Trust beaches over the years. It spoils the landscape and is devastating for wildlife. If the amount of litter on our beaches is an issue that concerns you, visit the National Trust website to find out what you can do to help.

SUNSET BELL

Legend has it that Pokehouse Wood near **Croft Castle**, Herefordshire, was the haunt of the notoriously mischievous imp Puck, who delighted in leading travellers astray. One local was so worried by what Puck might do that he paid for the church bell at Aymestrey to be rung every evening just before sunset to warn anyone in the woods that darkness was approaching.

SMALL BEGINNINGS 2

In 1899 the National Trust purchased 2 acres of **Wicken Fen** in Cambridgeshire for £10, making it the Trust's first nature reserve. Today it covers around 1,980 acres.

STRANGE TERN OF EVENTS

On 28 June 1980, a young National Trust ranger on the **Farne Islands** in Northumberland ringed an Arctic tern chick, released it and thought no more about it – it was one among many. Fast-forward to 2010 and John Walton was by then the Trust's property manager on the islands. When a veteran tern had its ring checked it was found to be the same bird from 30 years before, making it (at the time) the UK's oldest-known Arctic tern. When John heard the news he said he was 'out like a shot' to view the bird that, despite having covered an estimated million miles, still looked in good condition. *The Guardian* reported John as admitting, 'In contrast, I have led a relatively sedentary existence [but] alongside the tern I look knackered.'

*The number of birds ringed by the **Wicken Fen** bird ringers in the 50 years from 1968–2018.*

HE'S A BIG CHAP!

Right, it can't be put off any longer. It's time to talk about one of the most risqué items in the Trust's care – the **Cerne Abbas Giant** in Dorset. It's a massive male figure cut into the chalk hillside, around 55m (180ft) tall, not including his enormous weapon – this being the huge club he's wielding over his head. After much debate about the age of the monument (the first documented record of it dates from only 1694), in 2021 archaeologists declared that based on sediment samples, the likely date of its creation was from AD 700–1100. The giant takes about four or five days every year to maintain, then every seven years the chalk is replaced. The Giant had a nose job in 1993 to correct years of erosion. And that's all you need to know about him. Oh, and by the way, he isn't wearing any clothes; and he's definitely a man.

SOOTY'S COMING HOME

In 1966, when England won the football World Cup, a sooty tern, who normally prefers the heat of the Seychelles to the more bracing weather of Northumberland, was first seen in the **Farne Islands**. There were a few more sightings of sooty terns in the UK up until 2005, but never in the Farnes until 2018, just days before England's World Cup semi-final against Croatia. A good omen, surely, and the tern was rapidly dubbed 'Gareth' in honour of the team's waistcoated manager. Alas, no. Normal service was resumed and England lost.

THE RED LADY OF PAVILAND

When William Buckland found a headless skeleton surrounded by artefacts in **Paviland Cave** on the Gower Peninsula in 1823, it was stained with red ochre and he believed it to be female, probably from Roman times – hence it was dubbed 'The Red Lady'. But as archaeological knowledge and techniques developed, it was established that the remains belonged to a 34,000-year-old male, making it the oldest known ceremonial burial site in Western Europe.

CAVE DWELLERS

When you think of the word 'caveman' you may well imagine an image of a hairy, primitive, prehistoric human – like the inhabitants of Gough's Cave in **Cheddar Gorge**, Somerset, whom archaeologists have shown indulged in a spot of Stone Age cannibalism – but most people in 20th-century Kinver weren't

like that at all. And there were people living in the **Kinver Rock Houses,** Staffordshire, until the 1960s. The homes, tunnelled out of the soft sandstone of Kinver Edge, made quite cosy places to live for local workers: cool in summer and warm in winter. Some later had gas piped in when one of the residents, who worked at the local gasometer, laid his own pipeline. The 1861 census recorded 11 families living there in three levels of caves.

GOING DOWN

Here are just a few of the Trust's spectacular waterfalls:

28m (92ft)	Whitelady Waterfall, **Lydford Gorge,** Devon
27m (88ft)	Henryd Falls, **Brecon Beacons,** Powys
20m (65ft)	**Aira Force,** Cumbria
18m (60ft)	Rhaeadr Ddu, **South Snowdonia**
9m (30ft)	**Glenoe,** Country Antrim

PETER LABILLIERE (1725-1800)

If you take one of the many excellent walks around the Trust's Box Hill in Surrey (site of the 2012 London Olympics cycling road race), you may stumble across the grave of this former army major. He became increasingly unconventional after leaving the service in 1760, agitating against the government and wandering around with his pockets stuffed with political pamphlets. As his dying wish in 1800 he made two last requests, both of which were honoured: he was buried *upside down, head first,* on his beloved Box Hill, and the son of his landlady danced on his (rather smaller than usual) grave. His strange interment was witnessed by a great crowd of curious onlookers, who were dismayed on the way home to find the only bridge over the stream had been dismantled by local youths while they were at the ceremony. Wet feet all round!

ANIMAL ANTICS

Jock

Jock was probably the most famous of Sir Winston Churchill's pets. The marmalade cat with four white paws and a white bib became so intrinsic to life at **Chartwell**, Kent, that when Churchill passed away, the family asked that a cat with the same features always be in comfortable residence at the house. The National Trust has honoured this ever since.

Wild Wessex

Thomas Hardy's dog, Wessex, at **Max Gate**, Dorset, was more a terror than a terrier. He would walk down the table at dinner parties, helping himself to food. After being attacked three times by the wayward hound, the local postman refused to deliver their letters. But, as the poet Congreve almost wrote, 'Music hath charms to soothe the savage beast'; Wessex would sometimes hold Hardy hostage in a room until the radio was turned on for him.

Blue Boy

This hyacinth macaw owned by Evan Morgan of **Tredegar House**, Newport (who you'll meet again later), was a foul-mouthed, aggressive parrot with a penchant for attacking bald heads.

NATIONAL TRUST TREE HALL OF FAME

Tallest

A beech tree on the **Devil's Dyke** estate, West Sussex, stands 44m (144ft) tall, making it Britain's tallest native tree on a National Trust site.

Oldest
The Ankerwycke Yew at **Runnymede,** Surrey, is thought to be around 2,500 years old, so it was already ancient when Magna Carta was signed nearby in 1215.

Widest
The Great Yew at **Shugborough,** Staffordshire, has a crown measuring 175m (574ft) and takes 15 volunteers two days to prune.

Girthiest
Or, in English, the tree with the widest trunk, is the **Florence Court** Lime in County Fermanagh, with an 11m (36ft) circumference.

Strangest Name
The *Karpatiosorbus admonitor,* a new species of whitebeam found in Devon, was first identified in the 1930s in a lay-by near **Watersmeet,** a National Trust beauty spot. A sign nailed to it led to the tree finally being given its common (and, at the same time, rather unusual) name in 2009 – the No Parking Whitebeam.

OH, RATS!
When Beatrix Potter first moved into **Hill Top** in Cumbria she found she had company. Spotting 96 rats in two years gave her the inspiration for a story about Samuel Whiskers, though she took the name from her long-dead pet rat, Sammy. You can still see holes in the doors and floors made by the ravaging rodents.

MICRO-MANAGING ANTS
You've heard of ringing birds and microchipping mammals, but how do you put a tracking device on an ant? Well, starting in 2012, researchers from York University stuck tiny

radio receivers (1mm long) on a thousand of the estimated 50 million hairy wood ants at the Trust's **Longshaw Estate** in Derbyshire to study their behaviour. The findings helped rangers to be able to manage the ancient woodland in a way that benefitted these fascinating, hard-working insects. And if you think the northern hairy wood ant is a strange name, National Trust properties are home to other intriguingly named insects, such as the phantom hoverfly, the wart-biter cricket and the kiss-me-slow weevil.

IS THAT IT?

The 13th-century **Sharow Cross** near Ripon, North Yorkshire, is probably the smallest 'property' in the care of the Trust. It's Grade II listed, and consists of a base measuring 80 × 60cm (31 × 23in) with a short stub protruding – all that's left of the cross. There were originally eight such crosses, marking the 'sanctuary' limits within a mile of what is now Ripon Cathedral, and this is the only one that remains.

WHISTLING SANDS

We all know the annoying sound made by squeaky sandals, but if you're having a stroll on the beach at **Porthor** on Wales's Llŷn Peninsula, it might not make any difference whether you're wearing them or not. In certain conditions, the unusual-shaped sand particles on this beach can produce their own squeak or whistle when trodden on.

LET THERE BE LIGHT

Among the National Trust's nine lighthouses are two that were landmarks in the use of electric light. In 1858, the **South Foreland Lighthouse**, Kent, became the first lighthouse in the world to shine an electric light after Michael Faraday installed a system there. Thirteen years later, **Souter Lighthouse** in South Shields, Tyne and Wear, opened, and this was the UK's first lighthouse specifically designed to use an electric light.

NOTHING TO SEE HERE

The mistletoe marble moth, found in several National Trust orchards, camouflages itself by resembling a bird dropping.

GUESS THE ITEM ANSWER

It's an acoustic mirror or 'sound mirror', operating like a giant concrete ear trumpet. In the days before radar they were used to detect approaching enemy aircraft. The curved surface would concentrate sound waves into a central point, and these would be picked up by a sound collector (and, later, microphones). Trained operators stationed nearby would listen in using a stethoscope connected to the collector, though the concentration required to make out the different sounds was so intense they'd have to swap every 40 minutes. Some were free-standing structures but the two at **Fan Bay** in Kent were carved into the cliff's chalk in 1915 and 1920. Once considered eyesores, they were buried under tonnes of soil in the 1970s, but now their historical significance is appreciated and they have been restored to their original state.

ROYAL CONNECTIONS

TAKE YOUR PICK

If you visit **Chastleton House,** Oxfordshire, you have perhaps
a one in six chance of seeing the Holy Bible that accompanied
Charles I when he was beheaded in 1649. It's not that they only
put the Juxon Bible on show once a week – it's just that there
are several other Bibles in existence that are claimed to have
done the same thing. Bishop Juxon certainly comforted Charles
on the scaffold – and was rewarded when Charles II made him
Archbishop of Canterbury on the Restoration of the monarchy
– but we can't be sure which Bible Charles carried with him.

HERE COMES A CANDLE TO LIGHT YOU TO BED ...

... and at **Coughton Court**, Warwickshire, you can see a
chemise reputedly worn by Mary, Queen of Scots. And perhaps
not just to bed, either – some say it was worn by her on the day
of her execution at Fotheringhay Castle in 1587 – but curiously
it is embroidered with the date 11 February 1587, three days
after she was beheaded, so maybe take that with a pinch of salt.

INTO THE KING HOLE, QUICK!

You've read about the presence of priest holes in English
manor houses earlier in the book (see page 8); well, the priest
hole at **Moseley Old Hall**, Staffordshire, came in very handy

when Charles II was trying to escape Parliamentary forces after being defeated at the Battle of Worcester in 1651. He turned up at the hall tired and bedraggled, and you can still enter through the same back door he did, and see the bed where he rested. But the next day a group of Parliamentarians arrived outside the hall. While the owner Thomas Whitgreave argued with them, and (eventually) persuaded them to leave, Charles was hustled into the house's priest hole, a space barely big enough for such a tall man, but one he apparently professed to be 'the best place hee was ever in'.

HER ROYAL LOWNESS

You'd have thought that if someone who wasn't very tall was coming to dinner they'd need a *higher* chair than everyone else, but that's not how Prime Minister Benjamin Disraeli saw it. Visit his former home of **Hughenden** in Buckinghamshire

and you'll see a set of 12 elegant matching dining chairs used during the visit of Queen Victoria in 1877. But not quite matching – one has the legs slightly shortened. This might have made it easier for the diminutive monarch – she was just 1.52m (5ft) tall – to sit down, but must surely have made it far more awkward for her to reach her soup …

BUILDING PLOT

The garden lodge at **Lyveden** in Northamptonshire lies half-finished today, much as it was in 1605 when the man it was being constructed for, Sir Thomas Tresham, passed away. It might have been completed by his son and heir, Francis Tresham, had he not died later that same year while imprisoned in the Tower of London for his part in the Gunpowder Plot to blow up King James I (although he died of natural causes, they still cut his head off and stuck it on a pike). And it might yet have been completed had Francis's brother, Lewis Tresham, not run up huge debts living a profligate lifestyle. But then we wouldn't have had this mysterious half-built Grade I-listed building to marvel at.

KEEPING IT IN THE FAMILY

In the early 20th century, two brothers of the Mander family of **Wightwick Manor**, near Wolverhampton, married two sisters, both Indian princesses. In 1912 Princess Pratibha Devi married the restless Lionel (who you'll meet again later) and in 1914 Princess Sudhira Devi married Alan; Sudhira would go on to promote Anglo-Indian relations and women's suffrage, which would have gone down well at the manor, as the family had been strong supporters of female emancipation from the 1870s onwards.

HOO GOES THERE?

Probably the oldest royal site in the care of the National Trust is **Sutton Hoo** in Suffolk. The latest theory is that the 27m (88½ft) long Anglo-Saxon ship that was buried there held the remains of King Raedwald of East Anglia, who died in around AD 625. Certainly the treasures found when the site was first discovered in 1939, including the iconic Sutton Hoo helmet, point to it being the resting place of a V.V.I.P.

MONUMENT OR FOLLY?

If you or I were to erect a great big obelisk in our back garden, the only thing we'd have to worry about would be a visit from the council to check we had planning permission (well, that and getting it through the garage). But when Thomas Wentworth erected the Queen Anne Monument in **Wentworth Castle Gardens**, Yorkshire, in 1734 he was making a potentially treasonous political statement that could have been very costly to him. Wentworth was a Jacobite, meaning he supported the claim of the House of Stuart to the British throne rather than the Hanoverian succession that followed Anne's death in 1714. Fortunately for him the authorities turned a blind eye to his monumental disloyalty and he died peacefully in 1739.

CHAPTER 4

EAT, DRINK AND BE MERRY

IT'S MURDER GETTING A DRINK IN HERE

The welcoming **Dolaucothi Arms** in the Cambrian Mountains, Carmarthenshire, run by National Trust tenants as a pub and B&B, has a dark history. Back in 1876, the local judge, John Johnes, made the fatal decision to renege on a promise he'd made to his butler, Henry Tremble, that he could have the tenancy of the village pub – Johnes became concerned that Tremble's wife was too fond of a tipple herself. Enraged, the butler shot and killed the judge in his own library before turning the gun on himself.

CHEERS!

The National Trust looks after 39 pubs across England, Wales and Northern Ireland, on or close to the estates and countryside it cares for, including **The Fleece Inn**, a half-timbered, medieval farmhouse near Evesham, Worcestershire. There are painted 'witch circles' by the hearth, which were thought to prevent witches from entering the building, and it hosts regular morris dancing sessions (what the witches make of that, goodness only knows).

WHAT'S IN A NAME?

The **Crown Bar** in Belfast, restored to its ornate 19th-century glory by the National Trust, including the attractive 'crown' motif in mosaic on the floor at the entrance, was formerly the Ulster Railway Tavern. The story goes that when the pub was taken over by Patrick Flanagan, an Irishman with Nationalist sympathies, his Unionist wife insisted on it being named The Crown. Patrick acquiesced, but put the crown design in its prominent location so that everyone entering would have to wipe their feet on it.

FIT FOR A KING

Belfast's **Crown Bar** (which we've just popped into) is a great surviving example of a Victorian 'Gin Palace'. These opulent, lavish public houses began to appear from the 1820s when the government started issuing licences to control the sale of alcohol. Although seen as vulgar by many, they were a big hit with the drinking public.

POP IN FOR A PINT

The Red Lion at **Avebury**, Wiltshire, is probably the only pub in the world inside a stone circle.

FOOD FACTS

In a typical year National Trust cafés get through:

- 3.16 million eggs
- 176,670kg (389,500lb) of cheese
- 390,151kg (860,000lb) of flour

That would make an awful lot of cheesy pancakes.

TRUST BOFFINS GO BANANAS

As the pandemic entered its second year in the UK, on 1 April 2021, Trust archaeologists revealed a bombshell – new Latin inscriptions found at **Chedworth Roman Villa**, Gloucestershire, suggested that the lockdown staple, banana bread, was first baked by the Romans in Britain nearly 2,000 years ago. And that's not all. Indications were that, far from eating it, those canny Romans used it as building material.

EAT YOUR GREENS

In 2019, the Trust-owned **Sticklebarn** pub in Cumbria became one of the first places in the country to list the carbon footprint of each meal on their menu.

RAISING A TOAST

In recent years the Trust has helped revive the ancient traditions of wassailing – ceremonies designed to ensure a good fruit (usually apples) harvest in the year to come. Normally held around the time of Twelfth Night (5th or 6th January), this annual custom can involve singing to the trees to wake them up, dousing their roots in cider as an offering, banging pans together to ward off evil spirits, or even – as shown in the picture below – hanging pieces of toast in the trees (whether to attract seed-dispersing birds or just as a gift to the tree, who knows?). It's a fun way to spend a winter evening, though.

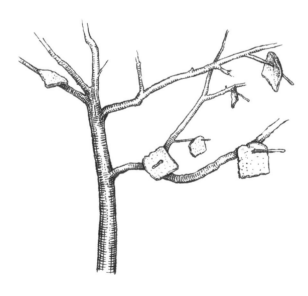

SIR FRANCIS
BLAKE DELAVAL
(1727-71)

The 'Gay Delavals' of Seaton Delaval Hall, Northumberland, were an 18th-century troupe of 12 siblings, led by the eldest brother, Francis. Their parties and practical jokes were legendary. Rumour had it that a four-poster bed could be cranked down into a pool of cold water to give its occupant an unpleasant wake-up, and there was a special topsy-turvy room where drunk guests would be put to bed only to wake the next morning to find themselves apparently on the ceiling – all the chairs and tables would be stuck to the ceiling and a chandelier would be poking up from the middle of the floor. Unsurprisingly, huge debts were run up by such extravagant stunts, so Sir Francis hatched a plan to marry a wealthy widow. He persuaded her to visit a bogus fortune-teller (really an actor friend in disguise) who told her she'd meet her future husband the next day in the park – and guess who was there to greet her. The marriage was not a happy one.

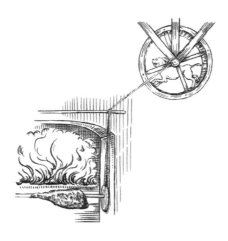

IT'S A DOG'S LIFE

A turnspit was a special breed of dog, now extinct, with short
legs and a long body, that would run around inside a wheel,
turning a cooking spit to help meat brown evenly. The one
shown here can be found at the **George Inn**, Lacock, Wiltshire.
The wheel was usually mounted high up on the wall, away from
the heat of the fire. The hard-working dogs were given Sundays
off, but only so that their owners could take them to church to
use as footwarmers.

TRUST EFFORTS BEAR FRUIT

The National Trust looks after over 200 traditional orchards,
the largest of these being at **Brockhampton** in Herefordshire.
Brockhampton has a whole 'orchard room' dedicated to the
damson, a tree whose numbers have been declining for many
years. This may be partly due to changing tastes and partly to
how long it takes the trees to mature. There is an old saying
that goes: 'The man who plants plums, plants for his sons; the
man who plant damsons, plants for his grandsons.'

WELL, SLACK-MA-GIRDLE!

In 2016 the Trust became the guardian of the National Cider Apple Collection, including such rare varieties as Slack-ma-Girdle, Netherton Late Blower and Billy Down Pippin. Each specimen was planted at two different locations out of eight sites, to increase protection against disease and help to secure the future of the UK's old cider apple varieties. It's hoped the trees will begin producing fruit in the mid-2020s, and the intention is to then produce cider from them. A fully grown apple tree produces between 50 and 150 pints of cider.

GUESS THE ITEM

Answer on page 88.

3,098,000

*The number of scones and cream
teas served at National Trust
properties in a typical year.*

PUDDINGS WITH CLOUT

In the early 1990s **Bodiam Castle** in East Sussex began hosting
one of the country's most extreme sporting events: the annual
Christmas Pudding Clout. For some 27 years archers gathered
in January to take aim at old Christmas puddings. Don't worry,
no National Trust puddings were harmed in this event.

ROXY MUSIC AT GLASTONBURY

In 1982, Roxy Music released the album *Avalon*, inspired by
King Arthur's mythical island. You might be disappointed
to hear that, good though they are, Bryan Ferry's songs don't
make a single mention of apples. Didn't someone tell him that
Avalon means 'island of apples'? And Avalon is the former
name of **Glastonbury Tor**, Somerset, where the Trust has
several heritage apple orchards.

10 WEIRD AND WONDERFUL APPLE NAMES

- Hangy Down
- Ten Commandments
- Hoary Morning
- Dog's Snout
- Pig's Nose Pippin
- Mevagissey Pitcher
- Cornish Honeypinnick
- Limberlimb
- Tremlett's Bitter
- Cider Lady's Finger

TROUBLE AT T'MILL

Apparently, when the Trust was restoring **White Mill** in Dorset, while clearing the undergrowth it came across dozens of empty bottles of chest medicine, presumably used by workers afflicted by the fine dust created in flour mills.

OLDEST TRUST VOLUNTEER

In January 2018 Joan Capel celebrated her 100th birthday; she was born when the National Trust itself had been active for less than a quarter of a century. And, like the Trust, Joan was still going strong, continuing to volunteer in the bookshop at **Erddig** near Wrexham, North Wales. She was originally attracted in 1987 by the reputation it had for decent lunches. She had helped out in several roles, even starring as 'Mother Christmas' in the house's seasonal grotto.

PAID UNEQUALLY IN BEER

It was quite common in days gone by for beer and cider to form part of someone's wages. At **Belton House** in Lincolnshire they brewed their own ale for these purposes; male servants were allowed a pint at lunch, dinner and supper, while women had to make do with a half at lunch and supper.

A GRISLY TALE
Work 'below stairs' in large country houses wasn't just tough – it could be dangerous too. At **Calke Abbey** in Derbyshire, just before the First World War, young scullery maid Gertrude Hopkins was plucking a goose. This involved singeing the bird over a tray of lit methylated spirits. Exactly what happened remains a mystery, for Gertrude was alone at the time, but her screams brought everyone running to the kitchen, where they found the poor girl alight from head to foot. She was covered in rugs to douse the flames but died shortly afterwards.

NO NASTY NIFFS
If you think many of the dining rooms at Trust properties look a little bare and devoid of soft furnishings compared to the rest of the house, you'd be right. Such materials were thought to harbour the smell of stale food.

WIBBLE-WOBBLE
Eighteenth- and 19th-century banqueters had a bit of a jelly obsession. There are hundreds of jelly moulds catalogued in the Trust's online collection, including this beauty from **Tyntesfield** in North Somerset.

WHATEVER YOU DO, DON'T SPILL YOUR DRINK

Julius Drewe, owner of the last castle to be built in this country, **Castle Drogo** in Devon, was very proud of his gadgets: he had an electric tea-cup warmer to keep his cuppa at just the right temperature, a luxury bathroom with a multi-function shower that soaked you from all angles and doubled as a bath, and a telephone exchange in the butler's pantry from where he could direct incoming calls to one of the 18 telephones in the house. The most worrying innovation was probably the candlesticks on his dining table, powered by an electric undercloth. Hmm, what could possibly go wrong?

FAIR EXCHANGE

The land around **Formby Point** on Merseyside was once famous for its asparagus fields. Formby asparagus would be sent by train to Liverpool, and in return the city would ship its 'night soil' (human excrement, to be blunt) for use as fertiliser. Yummy …

TABLE D'HÔTE

'Host's table' menus (with a fixed 'like it or lump it' choice) were all the rage in Victorian country houses, and you'll find samples dotted around several of the grander Trust properties. Perhaps we could launch a revival? These are all standard English fare, some of which sound a lot more appetising in French – can you work out what they are?

- *Boeuf bouilli et carottes*
- *Tarte et purée*
- *Haricots pain grillé*
- *Pain égouttage*
- *Sandwich au boeuf salé*
- *Dinde dinosaur avec pommes frites*

Answers:
- Boiled beef and carrots
- Pie and mash
- Beans on toast
- Bread and dripping
- Corned beef sandwich
- Turkey dinosaurs with chips

UNUSUAL NATIONAL TRUST JOBS

CIDER MAKER

Fair enough, this isn't the most unlikely job to find given how many apple orchards the Trust looks after. But how could we not mention the person who until recently was the chief cider maker at Barrington Court in Somerset? In a classic case of nominative determinism, step forward Rachel Brewer. And before anyone points it out, yes, cider is fermented not brewed. But we couldn't find anyone making cider called Fermenter, okay?

WHO KNEW BETTER THAN MRS BEETON?

First published in 1861, *Mrs Beeton's Book of Household Management* was an instant success and a staple in Victorian households. It's perhaps unsurprising that the National Trust looks after more than 40 copies – but the one at **Smallhythe Place** in Kent is perhaps the only one annotated by a celebrated figure. Smallhythe was the home of actress Ellen Terry, whose marginal scribblings include a note on the plum cake recipe: 'never currants, but sultanas instead' (there's a difference?). She also recommended using carbonate of soda instead of ammonia, which definitely sounds more appetising.

WATCH OUT, INCOMING TREACLE!

When the National Trust came to restore the Liverpool home of photographers Edward and Margaret Hardman (**Hardmans' House**), it discovered what a propensity for hoarding the couple had. Along with old rocks collected on holiday, and boxes of mysterious chemicals, there was a tin of treacle so old that it had exploded – there was dried syrup all over the ceiling.

UNIQUE PLACES TO STAY

What better time for merry-making than a holiday? National Trust places have been available to rent since the 1930s, when enterprising tenant farmers began to welcome holiday-makers. Today the Trust has over 500 holiday cottages of all shapes and sizes.

Doctor's Orders

Heathland Cottages, Dorset: These rustic cabins with pine-clad interiors were once an isolation hospital, built in the early 20th century.

Stranded

Agent's House, Dorset: Situated on Brownsea Island, access is by boat only, so once the last of the day visitors has left, a strange peace descends – you might even spot a red squirrel following the signs to his nuts.

Breathe In
The Birdcage, Cornwall: At some points, the staircase in this Grade II-listed cottage is just 43cm (17in) wide. That's not the only quirk to the layout of this former cobbler's shop, which is also pentagonal.

An Englishman's Home
Doyden Castle, Cornwall: Perched romantically on the Port Quin cliffs, you won't get lost in this diminutive Gothic 'fortress' built around 1830 for Samuel Symons, a wealthy *bon-viveur* who wanted somewhere secluded to drink and gamble with his pals.

Room to Spare
Horton Court, Gloucestershire: If you want to spread out, on the other hand, this Grade I-listed manor house is the place for you. Alternatively, bring some friends – it sleeps ten. Possibly one of the oldest lived-in properties in the UK, the house was predominantly built in the 16th century, but the adjoining Norman Hall dates back to 1185.

Cosy Cottage Cuts the Mustard
Mustard Pot Cottage, Norfolk: Pretend you're the lady or lord of the manor in this cottage on the **Felbrigg Estate,** with its narrow winding stairs and octagonal-shaped rooms. Then wander down to Felbrigg Hall as if you own the place – admission is free if you're renting the cottage.

Dark Skies
Nant Las, Gwynedd: This former observatory is nestled in the Dolmelynllyn Estate in **South Snowdonia**. It's now a snug little pink cottage surrounded by miles of walking trails.

Clom On In
Pontbrenmydyr, Ceredigion: Why not stay in one of the last surviving Welsh cloms – 17th-century, stone and clom

(similar to cob) cottages. This one is on parkland on the edge of **Llanerchaeron**, and still has its original cow stalls, cobbled stone floors and smoke-blackened oak trusses. It's eco-friendly too, kitted out with air source heating and solar panels.

Feeling Peckish?
Shute Barton, Devon: The Great Kitchen in this manor house, built in 1380, has one of the largest fireplaces in Europe, in which two oxen could be roasted at once. Or, as pictured on the National Trust website, enough room to play table tennis.

One Down, One Up and Up and Up
Trelissick Water Tower, Cornwall: This four-storey Gothick-style tower, which has just one circular room on each floor, looks like it's straight out of a fairytale. But when it was built in the 19th century, it had a very practical purpose, providing water to the **Trelissick** estate.

Are You Receiving Me?
Wireless Cottage, Cornwall: Stay in this Grade II-listed, clifftop cabin and you really will be treading in the steps of a history-maker. This cabin, along with the world's oldest surviving ship-to-shore station next door, was set up in 1900 by inventor and engineer Guglielmo Marconi for his pioneering long-range radio experiments.

CAPITAL PERFORMANCE
The **George Inn** in Southwark is London's last remaining galleried coaching inn, visited by Charles Dickens, who referenced it in *Little Dorrit*, and perhaps even (in an earlier incarnation – it was rebuilt after a fire in 1677) by William Shakespeare, a local resident.

DOES THIS BREAD TASTE CHEWY?

Around 1900, the 18th-century **Lode Mill** in Cambridgeshire was converted from a corn mill to grinding cement – hope they didn't get the bags mixed up! There had probably been a watermill on the site since the time of the Domesday Book (1086), so it was good news when, after many ups and downs, it was back to milling corn in 1982, thanks to the Cambridgeshire Wind and Watermill Society.

LIMITED LIFESPAN

In days gone by, mills would only last around 200 years – the pounding of the machinery meant the buildings were literally shaken to pieces.

PROMISCUOUS DINING

Don't get too excited, it's not quite what it seems … Before the mid-18th century, the arrangements at dinner parties were for men to be at one end of the table and women at the other. Around this time, those oh-so-sophisticated Londoners began a new fashion of alternating the sexes, and it caught on. Soon everyone was getting into what was dubbed 'promiscuous dining'.

GUESS THE ITEM ANSWER

Although it looks like some instrument of medieval torture, it's actually a pair of sugar nippers from the collection at **Wallington**, Northumberland. When sugar first became available in the UK, from the 16th century onwards, it was not granulated or in dainty little cubes, but came in a stonking great sugarloaf. These could be as high as 76cm (30in) and weigh up to 16kg (just over 35lb), so something fairly substantial was required to break off the sugar you needed, and that's where the nippers came in.

TOP TEN TRUST TOILETS

Here's the moment you've all been waiting for with bated breath (or possibly with crossed legs). Inside or outside, upstairs or downstairs or in her Lady's chamber, the National Trust has some pretty interesting loos. Here's a countdown to the top ten and, before you ask, no, you can't use them – with one famously named exception …

10 Thunderboxes Are Go

Thunderboxes were portable toilets and usually pretty simple: wooden stalls with holes cut in the lid that, once used, you'd shovel earth in. They can be found at a number of National Trust locations, including **Calke Abbey** in Derbyshire and **Snowshill Manor** in Gloucestershire.

9 When You've Got to Go …

Before there was the Shewee, there was the Bourdaloue. As you will see at **Coughton Court**, Warwickshire, they were more discreet than a chamberpot and designed to fit a woman's anatomy, with a lip at one end and a handle at the other. They bore a distinct resemblance to a gravy boat. It's said they were named after a Jesuit preacher, Louis Bourdaloue, whose sermons were so long that ladies needed a way to relieve themselves without leaving their pew.

8 The Royal Wee?

A 'close stool' or 'stool of easement' was an early form of toilet in the shape of a box with a lid and a chamberpot inside. The luscious, crimson velvet-covered one at **Knole** in Kent, probably dating from 1660–90, has a domed lid and carrying handles, and is overlaid with braid bands and brass bosses. It's possible that the 6th Earl of Dorset acquired it while Lord Chamberlain to King William III, and if so it is thought to have been used by the King's two predecessors, James II and Charles II.

7 Garderobes

Before modern plumbing, the height of sophistication when doing one's business was a garderobe, which discharged straight outside, to be either collected for fertiliser (useful) or fall straight into a moat (less useful). At the crazily crooked **Little Moreton Hall** in Cheshire, the waste fell to a cess chamber, which was flushed out by water from the moat. It also has a garderobe tower, with the toilets on different floors, offset (thank goodness) to prevent accidents.

6 Styling it Out

Treasurer's House, York, was the first property to be gifted to the Trust complete with all contents, thanks to which you can see two cubicles fitted with Chippendale-style toilets, each with a bee motif and scrolled arms. One of these arms is much shorter than the other, probably to have accommodated some mysterious – and now-vanished – fitting.

5 Bluebottles Beware
The outside privy at **Peckover House** in Cambridgeshire, used by servants and gardeners, was painted blue to keep away the flies. Which makes you wonder why all picnic sets aren't coloured blue …

4 Right On Cue
When Sir Thomas Colyer-Fergusson bought **Ightham Mote** in 1890, he made a number of alterations, including turning the carpenter's workshop into a billiard room. Maybe he realised it was a frustratingly long way to the nearest bathroom, or perhaps Sir Thomas just had a weak bladder, but he also had a door inserted in the room that opened out onto the moat.

3 Silver Service
The ultimate luxury loo is surely a flamboyant George II silver chamberpot, engraved with the coat of arms of the Booth family, who owned **Dunham Massey** in Greater Manchester. Created in 1747, it makes up part of Britain's finest collection of Huguenot silver.

2 Ancient Lavatories
Completed in the 2nd century AD, the toilets at **Housesteads Roman Fort** in Northumberland are the oldest toilets looked after by the National Trust – and possibly some of the oldest anywhere in the world. Housesteads was one of 16 forts along Hadrian's Wall and home to around 800 men. You can still see the huge stone cistern, remnants of the raised platform they would have sat on and the channel through which rain and surface-water would have flowed to 'flush' the toilets. Back then there were no cubicles and soldiers sat side by side, perhaps sharing the news of the day. News wasn't the only thing they shared: with toilet paper a far-off invention, they used a piece of moss attached to a wooden stick.

1 Classic Crapper

This has to be at No. 1, if only because visitors to **Carlyle's House** in London, the former home of writer and historian Thomas Carlyle, have been known to experience the thrill of using a Thomas Crapper Venerable toilet. Sadly it's a more modern reproduction, not an original, but it is located in its own cosy garden outhouse, which *is* original – and, given the literary greats known to have flocked to visit Carlyle, those lucky visitors may well have sat inside the same privy from which Dickens, Tennyson and Thackeray once contemplated life.

CHAPTER 5

FUN AND GAMES

FAR-SIGHTED GROOM

When a thoroughbred racehorse with an unusual name at the stables at **Calke Abbey**, Derbyshire, developed laminitis he was ordered to be destroyed. But his groom pleaded for Squirt's life, and Squirt went to stud, siring the stallion Marske, who in turn sired Eclipse, considered by many to be the greatest racehorse of all time and a prolific stud horse – some 95 per cent of all thoroughbred racehorses today can trace their lineage back to him.* Eclipse was also the grandsire of Copenhagen, the Duke of Wellington's horse at the Battle of Waterloo. And all thanks to a sentimental 18th-century groom.

LAUREATE LOCATIONS

If you want to see where the *crème de la crème* of writing were born or practised their craft, why not visit these Trust properties that were home to poets laureate and Nobel literature laureates, who all had something interesting to say about subjects dear to the National Trust:

Wordsworth House, *Cockermouth*
Birthplace of William Wordsworth (Poet Laureate 1843–50) and his sister Dorothy, also a distinguished diarist and poet.

> *'Therefore am I still a lover of the meadows and the woods, and mountains; and of all that we behold from this green earth.'*

Bateman's, *East Sussex*
This 17th-century house was the home of Rudyard Kipling from 1902 until his death in 1936. He declined the poet laureateship

---

* Eclipse was certainly an extraordinary horse – on his death his hooves were made into inkstands, and there are supposedly at least five of them in existence. He was also painted by George Stubbs and his bones have been preserved for posterity in the collection of the Royal Veterinary College.

but was awarded the Nobel Prize for Literature in 1907 aged 41; he's still the youngest ever recipient of that award.

> *'Gardens are not made by singing,*
> *"Oh, how beautiful!" and sitting in the shade.'*

Shaw's Corner, *Hertfordshire*
George Bernard Shaw lived here from 1906, until his death in 1950, and his ashes are scattered here. He was awarded the Nobel Prize in 1925.

> *'No man manages his affairs as well as a tree does.'*

Chartwell, *Kent*
Sir Winston Churchill's beloved home, where he practised his bricklaying, enjoyed painting in his studio and dictated most of his history books. He was awarded the Nobel Prize for Literature in 1953.

> *'We shape our buildings; thereafter they shape us.'*

TWO'S COMPANY, THREE'S EVEN BETTER
Smallhythe Place in Kent is a Tudor house that, since 1929, has had a small theatre (the Barn Theatre) in its grounds. It was bought in 1899 by actor Ellen Terry, who gave her daughter Edith Craig another house in the grounds, Priest's House, to live in with her partner Christabel Marshall (Christopher St John); they were later joined by Clare 'Tony' Atwood and the three women lived amicably there in a *ménage à trois* for the rest of their lives. The trio – respectively theatre director, playwright and painter – helped Terry turn Smallhythe into a thriving and pioneering place for women in the arts.

JOYCE WETHERED
(1901-97)

Joyce, Lady Heathcoat-Amory, was the last member of that family to live at Knightshayes Court in Devon. When she accompanied a friend who had entered the 1920 English Ladies' Golf Championship, on arriving at the course, the courageous Joyce thought she might as well have a go. The 18-year-old won, beating the leading female golfer of the day, Cecil Leitch. Pioneering Joyce went on to enjoy a sparkling amateur career in the 1920s, before losing her amateur status when she took a job in the Fortnum & Mason golf department.

FAKE OR FORTUNE, FIDO?

Researchers at the **Stourhead** estate in Wiltshire took to Twitter on 1 April 2018 to demonstrate the clever canines who are being trained to sniff out fakes from originals in the Trust's art collection. The only hiccup in the programme was when one pooch made a run for it with a priceless painting in his jaws (they didn't say, but it was probably one by Bacon …).

MURDER MYSTERY MAYHEM

In the summer of 1956, the house and gardens at **Greenway** in Devon were littered with bodies after a murder-mystery party went horribly wrong. Fortunately, this was only the plot of *Dead Man's Folly*, the latest whodunnit from the queen of the genre, Agatha Christie. She spent her holidays at Greenway from 1938 until her death in 1976, and used various features of her home in three other novels: *The A.B.C. Murders*, *Five Little Pigs* and *Ordeal by Innocence*. An ITV adaption of *Dead Man's Folly* in 2013 was filmed there.

GUESS THE ITEM

Answer on page 112.

EVAN MORGAN, 2ND VISCOUNT TREDEGAR (1893-1949)

In 1934 Morgan inherited Tredegar House, Newport. (You may remember reading earlier, on page 65, about his parrot, Blue Boy – Morgan also apparently used to encourage the bird to crawl up his trouser leg and poke his beak out of his fly.) A convert to Roman Catholicism, he had various altars dotted around Tredegar House, and allegedly kept a portable altar in the back of his Rolls-Royce. But he was also a dedicated occultist. So when he moved into Tredegar House he naturally decided that the one thing it needed most was a Magick Room. What he came up with impressed his friend Aleister Crowley, the notorious exponent of black magic, and came in handy when Evan used it to carry out a 'cursing ritual' to get back at the officer who court-martialled him during the Second World War, when he let slip government secrets to two Girl Guides.

SABBATH SLEEVE

The moody album artwork for *Black Sabbath's Greatest Hits* in 2000 features the spooky water-filled graves at St Patrick's Chapel on the **Heysham Coast,** Lancashire.

SILENT COMPANIONS

Scattered around various houses in the Trust's care, for instance **Castle Drogo** in Devon and **Canons Ashby** in Northamptonshire, are 'silent companions', aka dummy boards. They are lifelike cut-outs of figures – servants, children, soldiers, animals. Were they to deter intruders like the cardboard cut-out police officers outside supermarkets? Mere curios and adornments, perhaps? Or did they have a more practical use – some show signs of being used for target practice or as doorstops. One theory is that they were there to make rooms look bigger – they were usually just under life-size.

SOMETHING IN THE WATER

There must be something about **Lamb House** in East Sussex that attracts writers. This Georgian mansion, which once put up King George I for the night when his ship was blown ashore in a storm, has been home to the following literary figures:

- Henry James (*The Turn of the Screw*), who just missed a place on our laureates list after being nominated for a Nobel Prize three times.
- E. F. Benson (*Mapp and Lucia*), supposedly the first person to use the word 'diddums' in print (1893).
- H. Montgomery Hyde who, among many other publications, wrote the first National Trust guide to Lamb House.
- Brian Batsford, a painter and designer who later became chairman of the family firm, Batsford Publishing.

- Rumer Godden (*Black Narcissus*), who wrote short stories, poems and novels, nine of which were made into films.

TELLING THE NIGHT-TIME

Children's author Helen Cresswell wrote *Moondial* in 1987 after being inspired by the sundial at **Belton House** in Lincolnshire. The limestone sundial shows Eros, the Greek god of love, and Cronos, the Greek god of time. The book was made into a TV series the following year, and much of the filming was done at Belton. You can get actual moondials – the trouble is, they're only accurate once a month, on the night of a full moon, and even then you need a cloudless sky.

A TALE OF LOST LOVE

While William Turner was engaged to poet and activist Hannah More (1745–1833), he showed his devotion by having her poems printed on wooden boards and attached to trees on and around the Belmont Estate, bordering **Tyntesfield** in North Somerset. Remnants of the boards were found by the new owners of Tyntesfield in the 1840s, 70 years after they'd been put up. Sadly, the romance didn't last as long – William postponed the wedding three times before eventually breaking off the engagement, compensating his fiancée with £200, which at least gave Hannah (who also campaigned for women's education and against slavery) the means to pursue her literary career.

WHY HEELIS?

Heelis is the name of the National Trust's offices in Swindon, and here's your chance to pocket some trivia ready for that next pub quiz (although, to be honest, you're probably better genning up on flags or chemical elements). It's called Heelis after one of the Trust's greatest benefactors, who left 4,000 acres of land and 14 farms – all in the Lake District – to the National Trust in her will. She became Mrs Beatrix Heelis in 1913 when she married the lawyer who'd helped her purchase a property in Ambleside, but you'll probably know her better as Beatrix Potter.

UNUSUAL NATIONAL TRUST JOBS

DOCTOR OF DANCE

Stuart Bowden is a dance instructor at Sutton House in Hackney, London. Known as the Doctor of Dance, he runs an over-55s dance workshop, part of the thriving community venture of over-55s activities run at the property for the last 20 years. The Tudor manor house was run down and dilapidated in the 1980s until being rescued by the Sutton House Society. As Stuart says, 'The spirit of Sutton House is rooted in the local community.'

KIM GOES TO THE SOUTH POLE

At **Wimpole Hall**, Cambridgeshire, is a much-travelled copy of Rudyard Kipling's *Kim*. As an inscription inside reveals, it made the journey to Antarctica with Captain Scott's ill-fated *Terra Nova* expedition to win the race to the South Pole. The book accompanied Apsley Cherry-Garrard, the expedition's assistant zoologist who delivered supplies to the food depot that Scott and his four doomed fellow explorers never reached, and six months later was part of the team that found Scott's body. Cherry-Garrard later wrote his own memoir of the expedition, *The Worst Journey in the World*.

LIGHTS, CAMERA, ACTION

National Trust properties are now used for scores of film shoots – they're ideal for capturing period detail and atmosphere. Here's just a small selection from some of the most-used locations:

- **Castle Ward, County Down:** *Game of Thrones, The Woman in White*
- **Dyffryn Gardens, Vale of Glamorgan:** *Doctor Who, Torchwood, Merlin*
- **Freshwater West and Gupton Farm, Pembrokeshire:** *Harry Potter and the Deathly Hallows (Parts 1 & 2), Robin Hood*
- **Fountains Abbey and Studley Royal Water Garden, North Yorkshire:** *The History Boys, The Secret Garden, Omen III: The Final Conflict*
- **Great Chalfield Manor, Wiltshire:** *Robin of Sherwood, The Other Boleyn Girl, Wolf Hall, Poldark*
- **Ham House, Richmond:** *The Young Victoria, Spice World, Sense and Sensibility, Downton Abbey*
- **Knole, Kent:** *Pirates of the Caribbean: On Stranger Tides, Sherlock Holmes: Game of Shadows, The Favourite*
- **Lacock Abbey, Wiltshire:** *Harry Potter and the Philosopher's Stone, Pride and Prejudice, The Hollow Crown, His Dark Materials*
- **Ashridge Estate, Hertfordshire:** *The Dirty Dozen, Hot Fuzz, Les Misérables*
- **Osterley Park and House, London:** *The Dark Knight Rises, Miss Potter, Mrs Brown, The Crown*

MR DARCY (FINALLY) EMERGES FROM THE LAKE

In July 2013, a 3.6m (12ft) fibreglass statue of Mr Darcy from Jane Austen's *Pride and Prejudice*, as famously depicted by a dripping-wet Colin Firth, was installed as a temporary feature in the lake at **Lyme**, Cheshire, where some of the 1995 BBC adaptation was filmed. Several months later it was still there, but the National Trust of Australia had offered to give it a permanent home. Now all that remained was to somehow remove Mr Darcy from the waters where he was firmly and happily lodged. The intrepid volunteers of the Peak District Mountain Rescue were not deterred, though, and stepped in to liberate him.

HOW TO SPEND A FORTUNE

Henry Paget, 5th Marquess of Anglesey, inherited the family seat at **Plas Newydd** aged 23 in 1898, together with other estates dotted around the country. Less than seven years later he was dead of pneumonia and tuberculosis, having squandered much of the vast family fortune and been personally declared bankrupt. A devotee of the stage, the 'Dancing Marquess' converted the family chapel at Plas Newydd into a theatre, spent untold thousands on extravagant costumes and staged lavish productions, taking leading roles himself. Other extravagances included a collection of poodles and a motor car that had been modified to convert the smelly exhaust fumes into a fragrant scent. Upon his bankruptcy, he professed himself baffled at how he had got through his fortune … after all, he was only spending a mere £3,000 a year on gold-weave underwear. The Paget family were probably embarrassed by his profligacy; all Henry's personal papers were destroyed, and the 6th Marquess restored the chapel.

TREADING THE BOARDS

The **Theatre Royal Bury St Edmunds**, which opened in 1819, is the third-oldest theatre in the country, and the only surviving Regency playhouse. It's been in the care of the National Trust since the 1970s and is run by Theatre Royal.

WHEN I GET HOME

Two of the National Trust's later (and most recently built) acquisitions are modest family homes in Liverpool's suburbs: 'Mendips', also known as 251 Menlove Avenue, and 20 Forthlin Road. Architecturally unassuming they may be, but as the childhood homes of Beatles legends John Lennon and Sir Paul McCartney respectively, and the place where dozens of hits were written, culturally priceless.

One of the earliest songs Paul wrote at Forthlin Road was a cheery ditty called 'Suicide'; years later, when he was famous, Frank Sinatra asked Paul for a song and Macca sent him that one. Ol' Blue Eyes was not impressed, leaving Paul to admit, 'Maybe I should have changed it a bit to send to him.'

CURIOUS CHARACTERS

MILES
MANDER
(1888-1946)

Lionel Henry Mander of Wightwick Manor was a born adventurer. He tried his hand at motor-racing, aeroplanes and hot-air balloons; he fought in the First World War, married an Indian princess and dabbled in sheep-farming in New Zealand before changing his name to Miles and settling on a career in the fledgling motion-picture business. He specialised in playing English cads and smarmy villains – a kind of prototype Terry-Thomas – and moved to Hollywood in the 1930s, eventually appearing in over a hundred films.

LENNON VS McCARTNEY

If you visit the two houses just mentioned, you may wonder why Mendips has an English Heritage Blue Plaque, while Forthlin Road hasn't. Well, under the criteria for the honour, the recipient has to have been dead for over 20 years, or have reached their 100th birthday.

FROM BIRTH TO DEATH

The composer Edward Elgar was born at **The Firs**, Worcestershire, but the family moved after only two years and he would live in over 20 different houses during his lifetime, most of them near Worcester (perhaps so he could be close to Wolverhampton; he is reputed to have written what might have been the world's first 'football anthem' – 'He Banged the Leather for the Goal' – in honour of the Wanderers' Billy Malpass). The property, now also known as Birthplace Cottage, was opened as an Elgar museum by his daughter after his death, and two of his beloved dogs, Marco and Mina, are buried there. In what was a sad year for music, three of England's greatest composers – Elgar, Gustav Holst and Frederick Delius – all died in the space of 107 days in 1934.

PAINTING PING-PONG

According to the autobiography of Patrick, 5th Earl of Lichfield, when he visited the family seat of **Shugborough** in Staffordshire as a boy, he would play table tennis solo and experimented with different surfaces – he declared his favourite to be a couple of 18th-century landscape paintings.

SO IS IT A GAINSBOROUGH OR A REYNOLDS?

A portrait of Susanna Trevelyan at **Wallington**, Northumberland, was painted by Thomas Gainsborough around 1761. Ten or so years later, fashions had changed and another artist – thought to be Joshua Reynolds – was hired to update the painting: the pose, dress and hair were altered to obscure a lapdog and large hat. (On second thoughts, maybe the dog had disgraced itself …)

Paintings in the care of the National Trust; and you can add 6,000 sculptures to that too. The very first painting the Trust acquired was The Grasmere Rushbearing, *by Frank Bramley RA, in 1913.*

LYME'S HIDDEN WINDOW

There's a painting in the Drawing Room at **Lyme** in Cheshire that hangs on a movable armature so it can be swung out, enabling you to have a peek into the Entrance Hall beyond.

REALLY OLD MASTER

A painted medieval screen depicting saintly kings and clerics, part of a huge art collection at **Kingston Lacy** in Dorset, is the Trust's oldest painting, dating to the start of the 14th century. The man who is believed to have acquired many of the property's artworks was William John Bankes, a tortured soul who was gay at a time when this was a crime in England. Having escaped prosecution in 1833 thanks to his family pulling some strings, a second charge eight years later meant he had to flee the country, spending the last 14 years of his life in exile. It's thought on at least one occasion he sneaked across the Channel for a brief visit to his beloved home.

'WHEN YOU'VE FINISHED, CAN YOU JUST DO THE CURTAINS AS WELL ...?'

Dust is pretty light stuff, you'll agree. You'd need 10 billion dust particles to have a weight of 1g. So imagine how much dust you'd need to collect to amass 1kg (2¼lb) of the stuff. That's how much dust staff removed when they cleaned the Gideon Tapestries in the Long Gallery at **Hardwick Hall**, Derbyshire. At 70m (230ft) long and 6m (20ft) high, it's also the largest surviving tapestry group in Britain. Each individual tapestry (there are 13 in all) is so heavy the Trust has to erect scaffolding to rehang them after cleaning. The tapestries, depicting the story of the biblical prophet Gideon, were bought by Bess of Hardwick in 1592/3 for £327 (about £128,000 today).

LARGE BOOTS TO FILL

You'd need a very tall principal boy to fill these thigh-slapping postillion boots, part of the costume collection gathered by Charles Paget Wade at **Snowshill Manor,** in Gloucestershire, and

donated to the National Trust along with Snowshill by him in 1951. They're 37cm (14¼in) long, which is about a size 20.

PERFECTIONIST

There's a statue of *St Michael Overcoming Satan* at **Petworth House**, West Sussex, that's big, and good. In fact, it's really big – 3.4m (11ft) tall – and really good. But then perhaps it should be, because it took sculptor John Flaxman nine years to complete. It was carved from a single block of marble, apart from the enormous spear with which the saint is about to deliver the *coup de grâce*, and cost the 3rd Earl of Egremont, who commissioned it in 1817, £3,500.

WASPS VS MOTHS

The conservators at **Blickling Hall**, Norfolk, have been having a bit of a clothes moth problem, not good for their fabric collection, and instead of resorting to mothballs (which are useless – how are you supposed to hit any pesky moths with those little balls, anyway?) turned to a more natural method, as reported in February 2021. They introduced tiny parasitic wasps, barely visible to the human eye, which lay their own eggs inside moth eggs. They also added pheromone tabs, which confused the mating cycle of the moths and resulted in fewer moth eggs being laid. You'd think all of this would just lead to a plague of wasps rather than moths, wouldn't you, but these people know what they're doing – the wasps just die off, apparently. Curiously, the Trust staff reckon part of the moth problem was a result of lockdown, as the lack of disturbance by visitors had created ideal conditions for the pests.

FOOTBALL CRAZY

Burnley FC are, unsurprisingly, the only professional football team to train at a National Trust property. They've used facilities at **Gawthorpe Hall**, Lancashire, since the 1950s, and in 2018 opened a state-of-the-art training centre on the estate.

GRACE AND FAVOUR

Henry Holroyd, 3rd Earl of Sheffield, was a massive cricket fan (the Sheffield Shield, Australia's premier domestic competition, is named after him), and he had a fine cricket pitch installed at **Sheffield Park**, East Sussex. It attracted some of the great players of the day to exhibition matches, and there's a plaque on an oak tree in the grounds that was hit by a mighty 'six' struck by the legendary W. G. Grace.

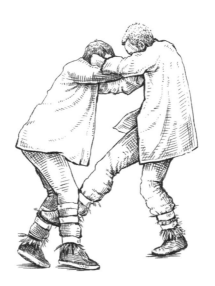

READY, STEADY ... KICK

Do you remember London 2012 and all that fuss about the Much Wenlock Olympics that began in 1850 and supposedly inspired Baron de Coubertin to set the whole worldwide Olympic bandwagon rolling again in 1896? It turns out the Baron should have nipped down to Gloucestershire for the truly traditional British version. The Cotswold Olimpicks are over 400 years old, and still take place at the original venue of **Dover's Hill**. The highlight of the Games is an event that graced the inaugural competition in 1612, the prestigious World Shin-kicking Championships. Little has changed over the centuries, but to reduce injuries straw padding is now in, and steel toecaps are very much out.

R.I.P.? NO, JUST F.I.P.

You can still see the visitors' book at **Bateman's**, Rudyard Kipling's home, and the 'F.I.P.' annotation added by the author next to the names of several of his guests. Can you guess what it stood for?

Answer:
'Fell in pond'.

GUESS THE ITEM ANSWER

If you said, 'Japanese porcelain incense burner', give yourself a point. If you said 'pottery insect prison', have half a point – it takes the form of a 'cricket cage'. This was a gift from Queen Mary, wife of George V, to socialite Maggie Greville of **Polesden Lacey**, Surrey, at Christmas 1920. A note attached says, 'this may amuse you' …

DOLLS' HOUSES

It turns out you were misinformed in Chapter 1 about Hawker's Hut being one of the National Trust's smallest properties (see page 8). *These* are by far the smallest houses the Trust looks after.

ROOMS BUT NO HOUSE

The Carlisle Collection at North Yorkshire's **Nunnington Hall** is a set of separate miniature rooms, crafted over a 40-year period in immense detail to the specifications of a Mrs Carlisle, who then donated them to the National Trust. Mostly replicated at one-eighth scale, they include such marvels as a readable (if you've got good eyesight or, failing that, a magnifying glass) complete works of Shakespeare and working musical instruments.

UPPARK

The 18th-century dolls' house at **Uppark**, West Sussex, built in the style of a Palladian mansion, is one of the best-preserved of its type in the country. The attention to detail is astonishing – the silver has minute hallmarks and the paintings are real oil on canvas. The tiny human figures are a bit of a giveaway, but otherwise you could convince yourself you were looking at the real thing.

NOSTELL

Another 18th-century dolls' house **(above)**, this is the only one still displayed in the house it was made for, West Yorkshire's **Nostell**. Such houses at the time were not considered toys. They were known as 'baby houses' and played a part in instructing the young ladies of the house as to how the household should be organised and run. They probably were used a bit for fun as well, though – after all, it's unclear what practical purpose Nostell's cheeky little glass mouse could have served.

HILL TOP

Beatrix Potter's former residence in the Lake District contains a dolls' house that has items reminiscent of *The Tale of Two Bad*

Mice, her 1904 book about a pair of naughty mice that trash a little girl's dolls' house before being caught and made to atone for their antisocial behaviour.

SALTRAM

Imagine having a dolls' house so intricate it has its own working snow globe. The 'Whiteway' House at **Saltram** in Devon is about 170 years old, and was donated by collector Vivien Greene (wife of author Graham Greene), who was considered the world's leading expert on dolls' houses. It also has a hand-painted paper-butterfly collection.

ALL MOD CONS

The Servants' Hall at **Wallington** in Northumberland has 17 dolls' houses on display, the highlight of which is the Hammond House, which has working electric lights and used to boast a running water supply. The same is true of the house at **Castle Drogo** in Devon, which also has a special gearing system enabling the front and rear of the house to be lowered into the base rather than opening up.

AUTUMN CLEANING

The two dolls' houses in the School Room at **Calke Abbey**, Derbyshire, are subject to an intricate cleaning regime every year before the house closes for the winter. Staff used to do it during the shutdown, but now visitors can watch the process as it happens. Each of the 210 items is inspected and dusted, which takes the team at least 15 hours. Using this as a bit of a 'warm-up', when they've finished they move on to a deep clean of the 'big' house.

SPOILT FOR CHOICE

Sudbury Hall, Derbyshire, home to the Trust's Museum of Childhood, is scheduled to reopen in 2022 in an exciting new incarnation as the Children's Country House at Sudbury. Fittingly, it's home to the Trust's largest collection of dolls' houses, 24 in all.

AND FINALLY...

If you really get into miniature houses, you might decide to expand your collection into a whole village. For inspiration, why not visit **Snowshill** in Gloucestershire, home of compulsive collector Charles Paget Wade. He created the model fishing village of Wolf's Cove here in the interwar years of the last century. By the 1970s the original buildings had become so fragile that the village had to be dismantled. In 2010 National Trust volunteers began the painstaking process of reconstructing Wade's Cornish village and today visitors can once again marvel at its miniature delights.

CHAPTER 6

HIGH (AND LOW) TECHNOLOGY

LET THERE BE LIGHT

Cragside in Northumberland was the first house in the world to be lit by hydroelectric power, thanks to the vision of its owner, engineer and inventor William Armstrong. Three years after lavishly entertaining the Prince of Wales at Cragside, in 1887 he became the first engineer to sit in the House of Lords, as Baron Armstrong of Cragside. Surely a coincidence!

LORD LOVE A DUCK!

The 3,000-year-old Uffington White Horse at **White Horse Hill** in Oxfordshire gained a companion in 2017, when it was announced on 1 April that a combination of aerial photography and geophysics had revealed another animal chalked into the hillside nearby – a duck. Staff speculated that these ancient giant artworks were originally prepared by competing Bronze Age tribes, with the survival only of the horse suggesting that the duck tribe came off worst.

NOT JUST HOT AIR

In 2014 the National Trust announced a scheme to change **Plas Newydd** on Anglesey from its most polluting property to its greenest with the installation of Britain's biggest marine-source heat pump. The £600,000 device pumps small amounts of seawater from the Menai Straits to a shore-based heat-exchanger, then up a cliff face to heat the entire 18th-century mansion, saving up to 1,500 litres (330 gallons) of fuel oil on the coldest winter days, making it not only a green scheme, but one that could save the Trust around £40,000 per year in running costs.

OPERATION WEED WIPE-OUT

Put that hoe down – it's time to bring out the big guns. When faced in 2017 with a determined foe like *Crassula helmsii* (also known as New Zealand pigmyweed), only the latest tech would do. The Trust didn't know for sure how the invasive species had found its way into the lake at **Claremont Landscape Garden** in Surrey, but it knew how it was getting it out – with the latest word in amphibious weeders, a cross between a hovercraft and a tank that removed the flora and allowed the fauna to filter through back into the lake. A massive 16 tonnes of pigmyweed was removed by two such vehicles in two weeks, and after that a regular six-monthly assault was mounted to keep it under control.

... AND THEIR LITTLE BROTHERS

In 2019, every Tom, Dick and Harry was helping with the weeding at **Wimpole Estate**, Cambridgeshire. Well, Tom, Dick and Harry were, anyway. They were a team of three robots developed by Bristol's Small Robot Company being trialled at Wimpole to see if they could be the future for tackling unwanted plants. Tom **(below)** digitally maps the terrain to identify the weeds, Dick destroys the weeds with an electric current (eliminating the need for chemical weedkiller) and Harry helps farmers plant new crops.

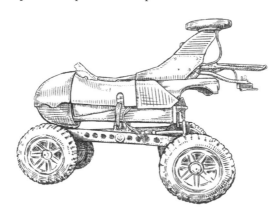

SPACE RACE ON A BUDGET

The **Needles New Battery** on the Isle of Wight is a fascinating place to visit, and was completed in 1895. (It's new compared to the Old Battery, which dates from the 1860s and doesn't seem that old itself, especially when you think that Newcastle's 'new castle' is nearly a thousand years old … where were we? Oh, yes.) After serving its traditional defensive purpose in two world wars, from 1955 it took on a new lease of life as a test/monitoring site for the British Black Knight ballistic missile and Black Arrow satellite carrier programmes. Black Arrow sent the first British-launched satellite, Prospero, into orbit in 1971, just before the programme was closed down, correctly judging there was no point in having any stake in these new-fangled satellite thingies. This was despite the Black Arrow being relatively cheap – when the Americans were told how much it cost, they supposedly believed there was a decimal point out of place, it was so reasonable.

A CLOSE SHAVE

It's a wonder **Wordsworth House** in the Lake District is still there for everyone to enjoy – the local doctor's family that lived there in the 1930s seemed to do their best to burn the place down. The doctor's daughter set light to her curtains with a gas light while reading in bed, and the family Christmas tree caught fire several times thanks to their practice of decorating it with real candles. Then, to top it all, the doctor was planning to sell the house to the local bus company so they could knock it down and build a garage when the good folk of Cockermouth purchased it and donated it to the National Trust.

HE'LL NEVER AMOUNT TO ANYTHING

When a young man left the family home at **Woolsthorpe Manor**, Lincolnshire, to pursue his academic studies having proved an abject failure at farming – he didn't even notice when his sheep wandered off – there were sighs of relief all round, with most sharing the view that he was 'fit for nothing but the 'Versity'. But what a fit he was there. Isaac Newton would, among many other achievements, go on to write *Principia Mathematica*, establish the laws of motion and gravitation (perhaps, or perhaps not, thanks to a falling apple from a tree at Woolsthorpe) and make huge strides in the study of optics. In 2017, Chris Pickup from Nottingham Trent University, used a special Reflectance Transformation Imaging technique to detect a new example of Newtonian graffiti on the walls of the manor house. Newton was well known for scribbling diagrams and notes on the wall to save paper, and this newly discovered drawing of a windmill could well be one of his.

TEN TERRIFIC TIMEPIECES

Clocks are probably the most common pieces of 'technology' the National Trust looks after, but how many do you think it has? And how many tell the right time? Find out after a rundown of ten of the most intriguing clocks you can find at Trust properties.

Pagoda Clock, *Anglesey Abbey, Cambridgeshire*

This golden tiered clock, standing 1m (3¼ft) high, is eye-catching even standing still, but once every three hours it becomes even more impressive. As the sound of a folk tune rings out over 12 bells, the three pineapple plants on each tier of the pagoda lift from their pots and spin. The scraps of newspaper and leaflets found wedged in the enamel (presumably to protect it from damage in transit) suggest it found its way from China to Cambridgeshire in the early 20th century.

Pebble Court Clock, *Canons Ashby, Northamptonshire*
There's a handsome blue clock face in the courtyard, but it's the mechanism behind it that has the fascinating story. The clock's original workings had long disappeared by the time the Trust acquired the property in 1981, so when the standard electric motor that powered it gave up, staff looked around for something more appropriate. Surprisingly, they found one on display in a Jaguar dealership of all places. It had spent 150 years from 1837 driving the clock at St Peter's Church, Eaton Square, London, until an arson attack sent it crashing 18m (60ft) to the floor. Written off by the church, it was expertly restored after a watchmaker's son at the scrapyard it was despatched to recognised its significance, and then ended up in the car showroom. What a journey!

Turret Clock, *Cotehele, Cornwall*
Good luck telling the time from this clock – it has no numbers on it. Come to think of it, it hasn't got any hands either ... nor has it even got a face. If you're lucky enough to be there on the hour, you'll hear it strike a bell, and that's it. But that's not bad for something that probably started ticking in the year Richard III was killed at the Battle of Bosworth Field (1485). Unlike most clocks of its period, for some reason it was never converted to take a pendulum, and until it was restored in the mid-20th century it had probably stayed silent for centuries.

Parliament Clock, *George Inn, London*
It was common for public houses in the 18th century to have clocks in them so their clientele could see what time it was. When the government of Pitt the Younger introduced a tax on clocks and watches in 1797 these public clocks acquired the nickname 'Parliament clocks'. The tax was a disaster, putting

clockmakers out of work and raising hardly any revenue, and was repealed after just nine months, but the name stuck. The clock at the George is a rare surviving example.

Courtyard Clock, *Lacock Abbey, Wiltshire*
Isaac Newton would like this clock, dating from 1880 – it's powered purely by gravity. Each week two great weights are wound up to a height, then as they slowly fall over the next seven days, they turn the clock – the right-hand one controls the time, the left-hand one looks after the 'dongs'. It rarely loses more than a minute over the course of a week.

Temperamental Clock, *Mompesson House, Wiltshire*
This is a curiously quirky clock that chimes with a minuet or a hymn every quarter of an hour. The clock also strikes the hour, but has a tendency to do so at the half-hour, or even the quarter … and it's been known to go an hour and a half between chimes. Still, what does time matter when you're losing yourself in a Trust property?

Harrison Clock, *Nostell, West Yorkshire*
John Harrison was born at Nostell in 1693, his father being carpenter there, so it's appropriate that it's where one of just three examples of his early longcase clocks is to be found. If you're thinking the name sounds familiar but you can't quite place it, Harrison is best known as the inventor of the marine chronometer, a device that hugely improved navigation at sea, saving countless lives in the process. His story was grippingly told in Dava Sobel's 1995 bestseller *Longitude*.

Round-the-World Clock, *Owletts, Kent*
If you're in the drawing room of Owletts and wonder what the time is in South Africa or Singapore, Canada or Australia, no problem. The remarkable clock above the fireplace shows the time in several different time zones of the world, and was created

in the 1930s for Sir Herbert Baker by his son, Henry, reflecting Sir Herbert's belief that the sun never set on the British Empire. In what some might interpret as a symbolic action, the clock stopped working in 2015.

Year-Going Clock, *Melford Hall, Suffolk*
This c. 1700 longcase clock was made by Richard Street – an apprentice to Thomas Tompion, the 'father of English clock-making'. Perfect for those in a rush, it only needs to be wound once a year and is the only year-going English clock in the Trust's collection.

52 Wrong Clocks, *Snowshill Manor, Gloucestershire*
Don't rely on the clocks at Snowshill if you need to know the time. There's one for every week of the year in the house, and not one of them is correct. Former owner Charles Paget Wade loved to hear clocks tick and chime throughout the day whenever they pleased, and so he intentionally kept them all telling a different time – and that's just how visitors to Snowshill will see and hear them today. The clocks are on show among thousands of other objects amassed by inveterate collector Wade, whose richly deserved motto was 'Let Nothing Perish'.

Answer:
The National Trust looks after around 4,000 clocks and a quarter of these are kept in working order – which means they (should) tell the correct time (unless you're at Snowshill Manor). Aren't you glad you don't have to change the hour on them every time the clocks go forwards and back?

CAN YOU BELIEVE YOUR EYES?
In 2010 the National Trust at **Knole** in Kent took a bold step. It replaced a whole room with a photograph. Knole has had humidity problems for years, and advanced systems

of humidity control form a vital part of conservation. But Knole went a step further. Over winter the Reynolds Room was stripped of all its furniture, paintings and carpets. The windows were resealed, insulation and a full-floor electric heating mat installed and a stud wall erected to make the room slightly smaller. Then the visitors were welcomed back in. Hang on, you're probably thinking, there wouldn't be much for them to see. Well, the new walls had been covered with a high-resolution 'seamless, vinyl, panoramic photograph of the paintings, furniture, walls, doors, fireplace and windows' to give an amazingly accurate representation of the room as it was before the project began. The Trust measured humidity levels carefully, and when the ideal heating conditions for the maintenance of the room and its contents were determined, conservation work began to transform the room. And vital information was gained to help the Trust at all its places.

UNUSUAL NATIONAL TRUST JOBS

SPOOFOLOGIST

The National Trust's April Fool japes that you might have noticed dotted around the book have proved so popular and successful that it now employs a full-time 'Spoofologist' to come up with new schemes. OK, not quite. But the team has certainly perfected the art of gently winding us up.

BANG ON TIME

This sundial from the Trust's collection at **Borrowdale** had a
little trick up its sleeve – the magnifying glass and small brass
cannon weren't just for show. If you placed a small amount of
gunpowder beneath the glass, then at the right time of day –
clouds permitting – it would heat up and go off with a 'pop'!

LOW-TECH SUNDIAL

You'd think a standard sundial is about as low-tech as you could
get. But someone's still got to find a block of granite, carve the
base, forge the metal for the gnomon, etc. At Buckinghamshire's
Ascott House, however, there's a sundial made entirely of
yew and box hedge. It's hard to tell how accurate it is, but as
a symbol it's beautiful; it was created to celebrate a family
marriage and around the 'sundial' is a motto, also crafted from a
hedge: 'Light and shade by turns but love always'.

SMELLYVISION

Secrets of the National Trust, presented by national treasure Alan
Titchmarsh, visited **Knole** in 2017, to interview scent specialist
Cecilia Bembibre, who was conducting research on how old

smells can be preserved. She calls smells 'the olfactory heritage of humanity', and has worked to preserve the smell of items like old leather gloves, books and even mould, with methods ranging from using special polymer fibres to capture chemical compounds, to just asking people with expert 'noses' like perfumiers, to describe the components of a particular pong.

GUESS THE ITEM

Answer on page 132.

VISITORS NOT WELCOME

Somewhere in Devon is a National Trust place not open to the public. In fact, not only is the Plant Conservation Centre (PCC) not open, its actual location is top secret, and it carries

out vital conservation and propagation work to secure the
future of countless historic varieties of plant, including:

- Flower of Kent apples from **Woolsthorpe Manor**,
  Lincolnshire.
- Knightshayes gentian, brought to **Knightshayes** in Devon
  by local villager and keen gardener Nellie Britton, and now
  dispersed over several Trust gardens to ensure diversity.
- *Eucryphia* 'Nymansay', a rare hybrid found at **Nymans**,
  West Sussex; the original shrub has died, but the PCC
  ensured there were descendants to take its place.

UFO HOTSPOT

You can't get more up-to-date technology than UFOs, and
many people reckon one of the best places to see them is **Cley
Hill** in Wiltshire. It all kicked off in 1965, when multiple
sightings of strange lights in the sky came to be known as
the 'Warminster Thing' (they obviously had a way with words
in the 1960s). The reports acted as a magnet for ufologists
and spawned several books. Interest eventually waned, but
occasional sightings of lights in the sky and stories of strange

bangs in the area continue. On an entirely unrelated note, Cley Hill just happens to be within a few miles of the Ministry of Defence firing range on Salisbury Plain …

Kilos of bird droppings removed by a specialist firm of pigeon-purgers brought in to support the National Trust's award-winning restoration of Wimpole's Folly, an 18th-century tower on the **Wimpole Estate**, *Cambridgeshire.*

HISTORIC PHOTO

The oldest surviving photographic negative in the world is a picture taken of a window at **Lacock Abbey**, Wiltshire, by William Henry Fox Talbot in 1835. The negative itself is housed at the National Media Museum in Bradford, but you can see a replica of the 'mousetrap camera' used to take it at the Fox Talbot Museum at Lacock, which explores the history of photography at one of its birthplaces.

WHERE THERE'S MUCK ...

Tyntesfield in North Somerset is an enormous Victorian Gothic Revival house remodelled in the 1860s and built on the proceeds of ... bird droppings. William Gibbs was reputedly the wealthiest non-nobleman in the country. He made his vast fortune from trading in guano fertiliser from South America. Chinese labourers working in slavery-like conditions performed most of the guano extraction. Before slavery was outlawed in Peru in 1854, guano was also extracted by some enslaved people, as well as convicts, conscripts and army deserters.

GUESS THE ITEM

Answer on page 132.

ELIZABETH
ILIVE
(1769-1822)

Elizabeth was the mistress and later wife of George Wyndham, 3rd Earl of Egremont, and they lived agreeably at Petworth House, West Sussex. They had nine children together between 1787 and 1803, although only one was born after they married in 1801. They separated shortly after their last child died in infancy. Elizabeth had a great interest in both science and the arts. It's thought she may have assisted J. M. W. Turner, of whom her husband was a patron, in the preparation of paints, and we know she won a silver medal from the Royal Society of Arts for her invention of a cross-bar lever, designed to lift large rocks. She also wrote a paper for the *Annals of Agriculture* covering her research into potato growing. It was published anonymously, possibly at the behest of her husband. Maybe that's one of the reasons she left him.

STRINGENT MEDICAL

Legend has it that the doctor at **Quarry Bank** mill, Cheshire, in the early 19th century had a quick and sort-of 'scientific' method of working out whether children were developed enough to be put to work in the mill. He would ask them to reach over their head and touch the bottom of the opposite earlobe. If they could, their 'reach' was considered long enough, and they were in.

GUESS THE ITEM ANSWER

If you said, 'olive oil container', congratulations! You can come and work for the National Trust. You're still wrong, however. This 17th-century pot was discovered in pieces at **Corfe Castle**, Dorset, in 1986, painstakingly put back together and identified as most likely being a kitchen item. But in 2012, a Dutch archaeologist saw it on Facebook and recognised it as a *stankpotten* or stink bomb, filled with noxious chemicals and used to clear well-defended rooms in castles under attack.

BONUS GUESS THE ITEM ANSWER

Well, if you do know, please tell someone at **Tyntesfield** in Somerset, because they're stumped. It might look like a skateboarding parrot, but it's beautifully crafted in brass with eyes inlaid with copper and silver. The Trust's experts know it's from 19th-century India, and it looks lovely, but why is it on wheels, like some kind of Trojan Parrot? (It's only 35cm/14in long, though, so you wouldn't get many soldiers inside.) And, most intriguingly of all, it's hinged and opens to reveal eight oval and spherical cavities ... but so far its use remains a mystery.

ACKNOWLEDGEMENTS

Dedicated to the memory of David Hall, who loved history, and Martin Hay, who loved laughter. I hope they would both have enjoyed this book.

Many thanks to Amy Feldman at the National Trust for her diligent research, without which this book would not have been possible, also to Claire Masset and Beth Snyder at the Trust for their vital input, and to all the volunteers whose stories have been included and those whose recollections had to be shelved for lack of space. Thanks to Peter Taylor and David Salmo at HarperCollins for their additional ideas, suggestions and encouragement; to August Lamm for her wonderful illustrations; and to Katie Hewett for her usual excellent copy-editing.

The National Trust would like to thank all of its volunteers and members who helped shape this book with their contributions. Special thanks to: National Trust volunteers Gill Laws, Ian Ross, Karen Kreft, Kim Prince, Malcolm Lill, Norman Monahan, Peter Kerry, Rosemary Segebarth and Steve Franklin; National Trust archaeologist Gary Marshall; and National Trust members Cathy Boyle, Clair Summersell, Darren Winstone, Geoff Franklin, Heather Parry and her grandson James, Martin Letts, Melissa Hookway, Mike Selway and Miles Franklin.

INDEX